Building a
Strip Canoe

Second Edition, Revised & Expanded

Full-Sized Plans and Instructions for Eight Easy-To-Build, Field-Tested Canoes

by Gil Gilpatrick
Master Maine Guide

FOX CHAPEL
PUBLISHING

Dedication

This edition is dedicated to all of the strip canoe builders out there who have used my previous edition over the past thirty years—especially those who took the time to contact me about their project. I learned from all of you and everything I learned is in this second edition.

Special Thanks

A very grateful thank you to Jason and Kelly Garland of Norridgewock, Maine, who worked diligently on the canoe built to illustrate this edition. They cheerfully put up with my frequent interruptions for photography. They are a great couple and a credit to the Maine work ethic.

© 2010 by Gil Gilpatrick and Fox Chapel Publishing Company, Inc.

Building a Strip Canoe: Second Edition is a revised edition, first published in 2010 by Fox Chapel Publishing Company, Inc. The patterns contained herein are copyrighted by the author. Readers may make copies of these patterns for personal use. The patterns themselves, however, are not to be duplicated for resale or distribution under any circumstances. Any such copying is a violation of copyright law.

ISBN 978-1-56523-483-3

Library of Congress Cataloging-in-Publication Data

Gilpatrick, Gil.
  Building a strip canoe/ by gil gilpatrick. -- 2nd ed.
      p. cm.
  Includes index.
  ISBN 978-1-56523-483-3
  1. Canoes and canoeing. 2. Boatbuilding. I. Title.
  VM353.G54 2010
  623.82'9--dc22

                    2010012470

To learn more about the other great books from Fox Chapel Publishing, or to find a retailer near you, call toll-free 800-457-9112 or visit us at *www.FoxChapelPublishing.com.*

Note to Authors: We are always looking for talented authors to write new books in our area of woodworking, design, and related crafts. Please send a brief letter describing your idea to Acquisition Editor, 1970 Broad Street, East Petersburg, PA 17520.

Printed in Indonesia
First printing: August 2010
Second printing: April 2011

Contents

Introduction

It doesn't seem possible that it has been more than 30 years ago that I sat down and wrote the first edition of *Building A Strip Canoe*. The fact that it was kept in print all those years continues to amaze me. The publisher was DeLorme Publishing, now DeLorme Mapping. As their mapping business grew and the book publishing went by the wayside, I expected the book to go out of print as each print run was exhausted, but they kept it going. Finally, in 2009 DeLorme let the book go out of print, and I was faced with the choice of re-publishing it myself, or just forgetting about it.

The book going out of print was just one of three amazing (to me, at least) happenings that led to this brand new second edition. The next thing was an e-mail from a former student, asking if it would be possible for him and his wife to build a canoe with me. I had nothing planned at the time, but kept his e-mail address. The final event leading up to this book was a letter I received from Alan Giagnocavo, publisher of Fox Chapel Publishing, expressing an interest in publishing my books. After looking over some of Fox Chapel's books, I was impressed and convinced that this was the right direction for me and for *Building A Strip Canoe*. These three events didn't happen all at once, but were close enough that I am still amazed at the coincidence of it.

A new edition was a wonderful opportunity to incorporate all of the little tricks, techniques, and ideas that have developed over the years and were not included in the original book. We did do updates to the book from time to time in order to keep up with changing technology. Some things could be added during those updates, but to do a complete job from cover to cover was impossible and impractical. With this new second edition, you will have the benefit of everything I have learned in more than 30 years of strip canoe building.

I have been honored over the years by calls, e-mails, and letters telling me how easy the whole strip canoe building process was to understand in my book. I think the main reason for this is the fact that I wrote a lot of the information, at first, for my high school students to help them understand the process. Later, a lot of that information found its way into the book. I realized that many of the folks who would use the book would not be seasoned craftspeople, but just people who loved the idea of creating their own canoe, and needed a little guidance to do it.

I have been involved in the building of more than 500 strip canoes. In the nearly 30 years I taught in the vocational center, we built them day and night. My regular junior and senior students had as many as three canoe construction projects going at any one time, and at night, I taught adult students who always had at least three under construction at any one time. Now the truth comes out, though. Until I retired and got a workshop of my own at home, I had never built a canoe all by myself! But I have done several since my retirement from the school system. Building the canoe to illustrate this book felt like old times to me. I had two "students" and I was again in a supervisory role. Actually, one of my "students" *was* a student in my shop in the early '90s. You will meet them both a little later on.

I have been in a very fortunate situation for a writer of canoeing and canoe-building lore. I had a supply of students who were anxious to help with the building, and were willing to put up with the endless experiments as I labored to make the canoes better, easier, and simpler to make. Then, when the summer rolled around, I had my canoe guiding business, where the canoes were subjected to just about every mistreatment imaginable. When I returned to school in the fall, it was patch-up time and also time to make changes that would ensure the next year's models would not suffer the same failure(s). I am retired from guiding now, but during my last few years on the rivers I tried out Kevlar for my stripper bottom. It worked out great and you can read about using it in the fiberglassing chapter (page 39).

I often got surprised looks from people when they realized I was going to use my beautiful strip canoe to run Class II and III rapids. I usually just smiled and said, "Yes, I am," and left it at that. But, I can give you a little more explanation. As will be explained in the fiberglassing chapter, these canoes can be made lightweight for ease in carrying or they can be fortified with extra layers of tough fiberglass and/or Kevlar to help them resist the beating that can result from hard use over shallow, rocky rivers. Of course, everything has a price, and the cost of added toughness is added weight. However, the strip canoes in this book compare very favorably, weight-wise, with comparable size commercial models, even when the strippers (canoes) are carrying extra layers of fiberglass.

There are no new canoe models in this edition. The eight models that have been included since 1985 seem to be serving well. The two E. M. White models, the lines of which I lifted from original wood-canvas canoes, continue to be the most beautiful canoes afloat, in my opinion. The Grand Laker is intended to fill the needs of fishermen, and others, who are likely to find themselves out on a large lake and so need a large motor canoe. They are not interested in paddling, but *are* interested in getting out and back safely. I am often asked if any of the canoes can be made with a square stern for motor use. Of course, any of them can be modified by squaring off the end, but the Grand Laker is designed from stem to stern for use with an outboard motor on large lakes.

My favorite small canoe is the Wabnaki. In it, I combined my own ideas and the features of a lot of canoe designs that I liked. I don't really feel I designed the Wabnaki, but I can't seem to blame anyone else, either. The name came to mind as a result of a lot of research I did on the Wabnaki (Abnaki) Native Americans for my novel, *Allagash*. The process of researching and writing gave me a deep respect for these people, and the canoe I had set out to make somehow reminded me of them and their canoes, so the name just seemed natural.

There are a lot of other great canoe designs that can be built using this construction method. Builders all around the country have come up with patterns for their own designs, or copies of classic designs used by great builders of the past. I have plans that have been generously sent to me that I just have not had the time or the need to build yet. The most

Start with **Chapters 1 and 2**. Learn what you need to know about canoe-making safety, and decide which of eight canoe models you want to build.

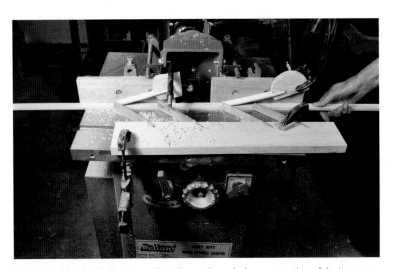

Chapter 3, The Preliminaries, will guide you through the construction of the items you need to build before you can start work on the canoe itself. Find the full-size patterns you need in the pattern pack on the inside back cover.

Use **Chapter 4** to learn how to apply cedar strips to form the hull of your canoe.

Introduction (continued)

common modification that builders want to make is to shorten or lengthen a model they like. This is most simply done by just figuring out a new spacing for the stations. I don't recommend changes of more than 1½ to 2 feet using this method.

It was only natural for us to turn to making paddles once we were well established in canoe building. In the early years, we used polyester resins; they did not turn out to be a good waterproof glue, and no other so-called waterproof glue did the job either. It wasn't until we started using epoxy that I was successful in making paddles that I deemed satisfactory. That was a long time ago and I am very confident in the paddles we make today. I used them along with the strip canoes in my guiding business.

It wasn't long after the first edition of *Building a Strip Canoe* that I learned white cedar, which has been a staple canoe building material here in the Northeast since the end of the last ice age, was not readily available in other parts of the country. As the book spread from east to west, I started receiving calls demanding to know where one could find this material. Well, the answer is that if you find it at all, it will probably be very expensive if it doesn't grow in your region. There are a variety of suitable woods that make a beautiful strip canoe, however. Western red cedar seems to be the most available nation-wide and it will make a beautiful canoe. For me the weight of the wood would be an important factor. The strength of the strip canoe comes from the fiberglass-wood-fiberglass sandwich, and so the strength of the wood does not have a lot to do with it. It does have a lot to do with the final weight of your canoe, however, and you will have to lug it around for a long time. We have built canoes from redwood, basswood, white pine, red cedar, and, of course, our Eastern white cedar. All have worked well.

The seat-making chapter of this book has been a popular one. I have had folks tell me they bought the book just for the caning instructions so they could repair the seats in some antique chairs. As simple as the wooden seat frame looks, it still requires careful craftsmanship and some good wood joinery to make the seats strong and long lasting. These wood joints will give you the opportunity to see what a great waterproof glue you can make with epoxy resin and cotton fibers, or some other thickener.

A large project like a canoe requires the accumulation of a pretty healthy pile of tools and supplies. At the end of each chapter you will find a summary of materials and tools to complete that particular part of the project. In addition, look to the Appendix for a source of the harder to find supplies and equipment. In many cases there are easily available materials and tools that can be found locally. Also, with a little common sense, substitutions can often be made.

Early in my writing career I subscribed to a writer's magazine, hoping to learn more about the craft. One day I read an article about how-to writing, which is mostly what I do. Leading a list of things the article author advised the how-to writer to do was, "never tell them everything." In other words hold something back for a future sale. My values rejected this kind of advice and I never renewed my subscription to the magazine. I vowed then and there that I would do my best to tell my readers everything I knew in the clearest language possible to help them complete their project. That is what I have done in this edition and what I will do as long as I continue to write.

Good luck with your canoe! I hope we meet on a river some day. Our canoes will be our introduction.

Gil Gilpatrick

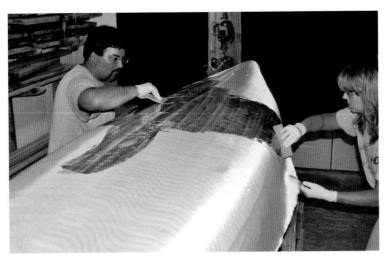

Embark on the fiberglassing of your canoe after reading **Chapter 5** thoroughly. When you complete the work shown in this chapter, you'll have a waterproof hull.

Chapters 6 and 7 illuminate the steps necessary to craft the remaining parts of your canoe—the thwarts, the decks, the seats, and more. You'll also learn to cane your own seats.

Construct the paddles that will propel your canoe after reading **Chapter 8**.

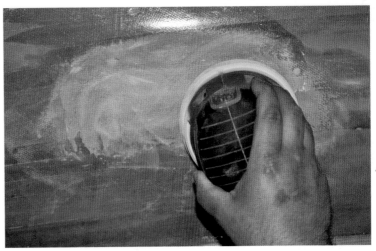

Chapter 9 walks you through how to make a repair to your canoe—an inevitable, but easily solved problem—as long as you reference this chapter.

Visit the **Appendix** for suppliers' contact information.

Contact me: I am glad to answer questions about your canoe-building project. My email is gil@gilgilpatrick.com. Please use a subject line that I will identify with canoe building. Example: *Fiberglassing my Wabnaki.* Since my email address is out there on my website for all to see, I receive hundreds of emails each week. If I don't recognize the subject or the sender, I delete the emails without opening.

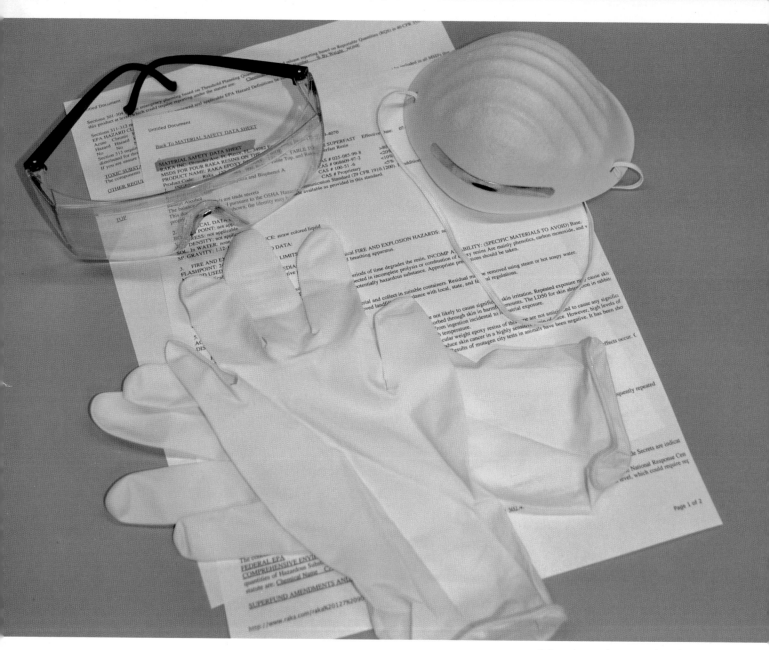

Safety glasses, gloves, a mask, and manufacturer safety data sheets are all necessary to maintain a safe canoe-building shop.

Chapter 1
Safety

To completely address the matter of safety in the use of all the tools and materials involved in building a strip canoe would make this chapter longer than all the rest of the book. Because such a long chapter is not practical or necessary, I have confined my safety remarks to only a couple of subjects that may be new to the average craftperson. These subjects are the epoxy materials to be used in the canoe construction, and the unusual amount of dust, from both wood and epoxy, that is unavoidably produced. I do urge you to use safe shop practices at all stages of your canoe's construction. As a former shop instructor who taught 16 and 17 year olds to use table saws, planers, and other dangerous machines, I am well aware of the need for safety instruction and discipline. Follow good safety rules at all stages of your work. Don't let an accident spoil this fun project!

Epoxy

Whether you are new or an old hand at using epoxy, I recommend that you request the manufacturer's Material Safety Data Sheets (MSDS) when you order your fiberglassing materials. The manufacturers and dealers are required to provide these to anyone requesting them. Because I have no way of knowing the brand of epoxy materials you might use, I have kept my comments on safety generalized in nature. Because I do not use polyester resin for strip canoe construction, nor do I recommend the use of it, I will not address those products here or elsewhere in this book.

I am indebted to the folks at Gougeon Brothers, Inc. who have allowed me to make use of the chapter on safety from their book, *The Gougeon Brothers on Boat Construction*, 5th ed. (Bay City MI, 2005).

Overexposure to epoxy

In more than 35 years of working with epoxy products, I have never experienced any adverse effects related to their use. I was aware of the danger of long-term use, and I took reasonable care not to allow the liquid resin or hardener to touch my skin. I was also careful to limit my exposure to the dust produced when partially cured epoxy is sanded. I did find that, once in a while, a student would come along who was immediately sensitive to the epoxy. They didn't need to get the material on their skin (although they may have without my knowledge); it seemed that just the fumes, which are all but undetectable, were enough to cause the reaction. These sensitive individuals numbered fewer than five in my nearly 30 years of teaching. Also, there occasionally were individuals who reacted to the epoxy sanding dust. Those people could handle the resin (as long as it didn't get on their skin), but broke out in a rash if they were even minimally exposed to the dust. The very few sensitive individuals that I encountered over the years did not cause a hardship—I merely kept them away from the problem.

A hazardous substance can enter the body by skin absorption, inhalation, or ingestion. Because I cannot imagine one eating the liquid material, I will confine my remarks to the skin and breathing. The risk of exposure to resin, hardener, and mixed epoxy is greatest when they are liquid. As epoxy cures, the chemical ingredients react to form a non-hazardous solid. The solid form is less likely to enter the body by any route.

Skin contact is the most common means of exposure to resins and hardeners. Even minor skin contact, if repeated often enough, can cause sensitization and chronic health problems.

Exposure by inhaling vapors is unlikely because epoxy products evaporate slowly. However, adequate ventilation is important because, if lacking, the risk increases. Also, the risk is higher when the product is heated.

Sanding partially cured epoxy produces an airborne dust, which increases your risk of exposure by skin contact, inhalation, or ingesting. Although epoxy may cure firm enough to sand within a day, it may not cure completely for up to two weeks. Until the complete cure, the dust can contain unreacted hazardous components. Do not overlook or underestimate this hazard.

Health effects from overexposure to epoxy

The health problems that might stem from epoxy use are dermatitis, allergic dermatitis (sensitization), severe irritation, chemical burns, and respiratory irritation.

I have worked with epoxy materials for more than 35 years, much of that time on a daily basis. Because of this I have had a much higher risk of exposure to epoxy than the builder who makes one or two canoes. By using common-sense precautions, I have avoided even the slightest health problem from epoxy exposure. However, as previously stated, there are those rare individuals who seem to be sensitive from day one. If you are one of those people, you should be even more diligent in protecting yourself from contamination.

Fewer than 10% of epoxy users react when overexposed to epoxy resin or hardener. The most common reaction is contact dermatitis, or skin inflammation. Both the resin and the hardener in liquid form, if allowed to come into contact with the skin, can cause this reaction. Also, the partially cured epoxy sanding dust, if allowed to settle on your skin, can cause contact dermatitis.

Allergenic dermatitis, a more serious condition, is possible from contact with epoxy resin or hardener. In allergenic dermatitis, the body hyperreacts to the material(s). Your immune system and the degree and frequency of exposure to epoxy affect your chances of sensitization. Gross overexposure, inherent sensitization, or an allergy to some component of epoxy increases your susceptibility. Other potential susceptibility-increasing factors include fair skin, previous exposure to other sensitizing substances, hay fever, other allergies, or stress.

Most epoxy hardeners are moderately corrosive. If left in contact with the skin, they can severely irritate it and can cause moderate chemical burns. The burns can develop gradually and first cause irritation and slight pain. When resin and hardener are mixed, the hardener is diluted and is therefore less corrosive. Even though the mixed epoxy is less corrosive, remove it from your skin. Exposure increases your chances of eventually developing allergic dermatitis. Also, epoxy cures rapidly in a warm environment so removal is difficult.

Breathing highly concentrated epoxy vapor irritates the respiratory system and causes sensitization. At room temperature, highly concentrated vapors are unlikely. However, if you are already sensitized to epoxy, exposure to low vapor concentrations can trigger an allergic reaction. Warmer temperatures and unventilated spaces increase the epoxy vapor levels. Do not inhale the sanding dust of partially cured epoxy. Epoxy chemicals remain reactive until cured. Trapped dust particles create the potential for severe respiratory irritation and/or respiratory allergies. Smokers and others whose lungs are under strain are far more likely to develop serious respiratory problems.

Solvents

Many solvents pose serious health and safety hazards. Some epoxy users commonly use solvents to dissolve uncured epoxy from tools and to degrease surfaces before bonding. I avoid using solvents in canoe building. Cleanup is easily done without them and degreasing is not applicable to canoe building. I recommend you avoid having those dangerous and usually highly flammable chemicals in your shop. If you do opt to use them, follow the manufacturer's use and storage instructions carefully.

Dust

Canoe building produces wood dust in quantity. We often think of wood as an organic material and assume it is benign. In fact, breathing quantities of wood dust leads to serious potential health hazards. Canoe builders using redwood or western red cedar, for instance, produce dust with adverse health effects. Using either wood requires familiarization with the potential hazards and ways to prevent exposure.

Over the years, I noticed I developed a mild reaction to dust from Eastern white cedar—my most common canoe-building material. In the school shop situation, where I had students working on a number of projects, it was sometimes impossible for me to wear a dust mask. If sawing, planing, or sanding cedar, I sneezed until removing myself from the problem dust. My reaction was mostly just an inconvenience and never developed into a serious health problem.

Safety Suggestions

The following sensible shop suggestions reduce exposure to epoxy dusts, wood dusts, and fillers.

1. Use personal protective equipment if you handle wood to which you may be particularly sensitive.

2. Sand only in an area with adequate ventilation. Wear an approved dust mask. Make sure everyone in the shop, not just the person sanding, is wearing a dust mask. If possible, and practical, sand outdoors where the dust will dissipate more rapidly.

3. If there is a choice, use a cutting tool rather than an abrading tool.

4. Use wet, rather than dry, sanding techniques on epoxy.

5. Vacuum your shop floor rather than sweep.

6. Use dust collectors on major dust producing machinery.

7. If you opt for solvents, take steps to prevent fires. Store the solvents safely and make rules about smoking. Dust, solvent vapors, and an ignition source can cause an explosion.

8. Prevent static electricity. If handling large quantities of dust or filler, ground equipment properly.

9. When handling fillers (cedar flour, cotton fibers, silica, etc.) keep them from becoming airborne.

Summary

There seems to be no end to the hazards of working in a shop situation. In the course of your canoe-building project, you will probably run a greater risk from misusing power tools than from using epoxy products. It is self-defeating to worry a great deal about epoxies if you are careless about using your table saw. Common sense is your greatest asset!

I hope that I have not scared you away with this candid discussion of significant hazards. While building a canoe, power tool misuse presents a greater risk than using epoxy products. With foresight, hazards are easily dealt with, producing safe working conditions. However, it is important to realize sometimes reactions are cumulative. Toxic reactions result from one cause or a combination of factors. While you might not react to any one of these individually, their combined effect might be hazardous. The same is true with lung problems. A combination of smoking and inhaling wood dust and solvent fumes could produce breathing problems, while no one of these hazards by itself might be enough to cause the problem. Precautions, good health, common sense, and safe working conditions are the best ways to avoid health risks.

Keep your shop safe and enjoy your canoe-building project!

This is Kelly and Jason Garland of Norridgewock, Maine, proudly showing off their brand new 18.5-foot (5.5-meter) White Guide Model canoe. This is the canoe that we built to illustrate this book. The hands in most of the photos, as well as a face now and then, are theirs. Jason was a student of mine back in the early '90s.

Chapter 2
The Canoe Models

Which canoe to build? Start out by considering how you intend to use the canoe. Will it be used primarily on a lake, a flat river, or in whitewater? Will it be used for lengthy trips on wilderness waters or just for daily recreation? This is not to say that a canoe designed for one purpose cannot be used for another; if this were the case, you would need a backyard full of canoes! The canoe is a versatile craft, and one canoe can serve you well. But, if you know how your canoe is going to be used most of the time, then use that knowledge to help you choose a design and size that will meet your needs most of the time.

Design Elements

The major differences in canoe design are shown in **Figure 2-1**. A person with a moderate amount of experience could appreciate these variations as soon as he or she had the canoes in the water. However, the various subtle changes to these basic forms that are possible would take an expert to detect, and miles of practical use to appreciate.

Let's look at the major considerations in canoe design, how they affected the choices of designs for this book, and how they will affect you.

Flat bottom versus round bottom

This is basically a question of stability and capacity versus speed. I am not into racing, so my canoes tend to be flat bottomed or slightly rounded. The increased stability is appreciated by the novice in flat water and by everyone in whitewater. There is a term, "secondary stability," you may see used by some canoe writers when describing a round-bottomed canoe. The idea is that a round-bottomed canoe, while it may seem initially unstable in the water, will actually be more stable after being tipped beyond a certain point. I cannot fault the reasoning behind this, but have found the information of little practical use and hard to demonstrate satisfactorily on the water.

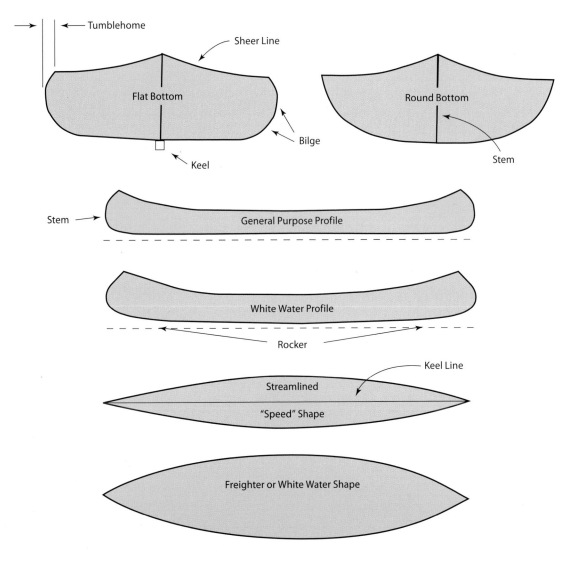

Figure 2-1: The basic canoe shapes and some canoe nomenclature are shown here. The illustrations are exaggerated to show the differences. Most canoes, including the ones in this book, are a compromise of these extremes.

Keel or not?

The **keel** keeps the canoe running straight, and so helps a novice in flat water. Many people believe the keel adds stability to the canoe, but I don't think it does so to any significant degree. What gives the canoe stability is the flat, or nearly flat, bottom found on most canoes that have a keel. The other thing giving a canoe stability is the experience of the user. When asked if one of my canoes is "tippy," I never know what to say, because I find no canoe to be tippy. A keel affords some protection to the canoe bottom if you hit a rock. Yet the added stiffness is of questionable value if the rock hits somewhere other than directly on the keel. The keel is a nightmare in whitewater! It makes maneuvering difficult, and adds to the depth of the canoe, thus decreasing clearance and increasing the chance of becoming hung up on a rock. If you are considering a keel because it will help you keep the canoe running straight, consider learning how to do the same thing with your paddle.

Rocker

Rocker describes the curve of the keel line from bow to stern. In short, the higher the ends of the canoe are in comparison to the bottom, the more rocker the canoe has. Canoes with rocker are generally recognized as river canoes. The upturned ends, in effect, give the canoe bottom a rounded shape, which makes it easier to turn. Think how easily a round tub would spin and turn—this is the theory behind that rounded shape. During the spring run-off in Maine, my wife and I often spend the weekends with other couples canoeing nearby whitewater rivers. On one of these trips, my wife couldn't go with me, so I took the 16 foot (5 meter)-long White Water and paddled solo. That

was a long time ago, but I remember how well the canoe responded to my paddle. It was almost like it was reading my mind. That is what a canoe with rocker does for you. However, the river canoes in this book are not exactly special-purpose craft. We used ours for extended trips involving both whitewater paddling and lake paddling. They were outstanding on the river and satisfactory on the lakes. Pick your canoe for what is most important to you; it will probably be perfectly satisfactory for everything else. Of course, once you have built one canoe, you will probably want to build another for the second most important use you have for a canoe.

Stem height

Stem height refers to the height of the tips of the canoe. This is a matter of personal preference and utility. The classic high stem, with all its gracefulness and eye appeal, probably evolved from Indian ceremonial designs, or from the idealistic eye of long-forgotten artists who took license with their work. However high stems came about, they are not too practical. High stems provide wind with too much surface. Most modern canoe designs keep the stems low.

Streamlined versus freighter shape

I think most canoes are a compromise in this department. There are racers using one extreme, and freighters choosing the other. The extra width in the ends of the freighter, or whitewater, shape give "lift" in whitewater. Lift is important when the canoe pitches down from one level to another. Of course, it means extra flotation for hauling freight or using a motor.

Canoe Designs

This book provides eight beautiful and practical canoe designs from which to select. Take into account how, where, and how many people will be using your canoe and read on to make your decision.

The E. M. White designs

"Mr. White, I made a mistake."

"Did you learn anything from it?"

"Sure did."

"Well then, it was not mistake."

This conversation between the founder of the E. M. White Canoe Company and one of his young employees sums up the employee-employer relationship that existed, and gives us some insight as to the kind of man he was.

E. M. White was born and reared on the Penobscot River in Maine and learned to love the water at an early age. His father was an expert paddle and oar-maker (bateau oars were his specialty), and the younger White built his first canoe in his father's shop in the late-1880s. Someone bought it on its maiden voyage, and the White Canoe Company was launched.

"Someone wanted that canoe more than I did, so I sold it, built another, and another, and I've been at it ever since."

White took the lines for his canoes from those of the Native American canoes that had been moving up and down Penobscot waters for countless centuries. It is interesting that the wood-and-canvas canoe that made the White name famous came into being not because it was considered better at the time, but because the large canoe birches were becoming harder and harder to find due to heavy use. More plentiful materials had to be found.

Just how closely the White designs follow the old Native American designs is hard to determine. After

White Designs		
	18' (5.5m) Guide	20' (6m) Guide
Length	18' 6" (5.6m)	20' (6m)
Width	34½" (.8m)	41" (1m)
Depth	12" (.3m)	13" (.33m)
Stem height	23" (.58m)	24" (.6m)
Approximate weight	75 lbs. (34 kg)	90 lbs. (41kg)

seeing more than a token number of old Native American birchbark canoes, I cannot say firsthand. I have studied photos of bark canoes, and it becomes a case of personal interpretation. Because you can only see one view from a photograph, you have to imagine the rest. Company records and written accounts suggest White's canoes closely resembled those constructed by native Americans. I have seen a photograph of several guides in their canoes, probably taken at Moosehead Lake, Maine, in the early 1900s. The wood-canvas canoes in the photo are unquestionably Whites. Some of the guides stood in birch canoes bearing a strong resemblance to their more modern counterparts.

The two White designs I have presented in this book are called "Guide" models, though I am not sure that designation is entirely correct. Not that guides didn't use that design, but early brochures loaned to me by the company indicate that a canoe was designated "Guide Model" not because it was a special design for the exclusive use of those woodsmen, but because it was "planned throughout for hunting and fishing…no money put into ornamenting…carried in stock painted drab or slate-color only." In other words, it was a plain canoe built for work, not for show. Your strip built White design will please both the artist and craftsman in you and at the same time stand up and be counted with the best of them when it

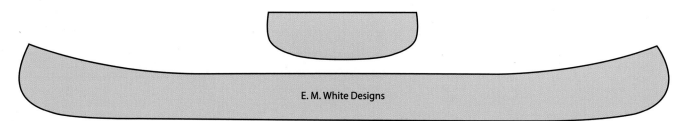

E. M. White Designs

Figure 2-2. E.M. White Designs.

comes to day-in-day-out work on the river. I tell you this with the assurance of long experience, because the 20 foot (6 meter) White design was my personal canoe for my guided canoe trips for over 30 years on the Allagash and other Maine rivers.

20-foot (6-meter) White Guide: Broad and deep, yet tapering to a narrow bow, the 20 foot (6 meter) White is a pleasure to handle with a load of 1,000 to 1,500 pounds (455 to 680 kg) or with just two paddlers out for a day's fun on the river or lake. The bow and stern may be a trifle high and cause for concern in a crosswind, but I have never found this canoe to be bad in this respect. For sure, I would not want to alter that beautiful sheer line that makes the White so recognizable. Just how important is beauty in a working canoe? Of course it is second to utility, but with the 20 foot (6 meter) White model there is no need to sacrifice one for the other. I highly recommend it.

18-foot (5.5-meter) White Guide: The 18-foot (5.5-meter) White Guide model is actually an 18½ foot (5.6 meter) canoe. Why this odd length was used is open to question; maybe it reinforces the claim that E. M. White copied the old Native American designs, which would have been made with measurements known only to them. I wish I had the words or the artistic ability to express the beauty I see in the lines of this canoe. Because I am a lifelong hunter and lover of wildlife, I can best express it in terms of deer. I think of the 20-footer

(6.1-meter) as a large, beautiful, and powerful buck. The 18-footer (5.5 meter) would be his smaller, more graceful, but just as beautiful doe.

These are two completely different canoes, and not a case where one design has been altered to produce another (except possibly by Mr. White almost a century ago). For the White Guide, you will do best to use the pattern for the canoe you need, and not try to modify. If you want the closest thing to an all-around canoe that is beautiful to look at as well as functional, then look no farther than one of these White designs.

20-foot White Guide Model. My best friend, Dick Mosher, and I have a wilderness camp with no road access. The old log cabin needed a new floor. We made a catamaran with two 20-foot (6-meter) Whites by lashing 2x4s across the thwarts. The "cat" easily handled the load of ⅝" (127mm) plywood, foam insulation, metal bunk beds, a generator, power tools, and a dolly.

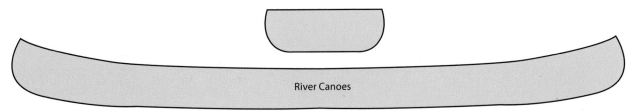

Figure 2-3. River canoe profile.

The river canoes

Whenever you look at the profile of a canoe and a banana comes to mind, you are looking at a canoe designed to be used in moving water. The Eastern Cree in Canada built a canoe that was literally banana-shaped, with a rocker that extended the entire length of the canoe. The modern rockered canoe has the up-turn for the last three or four feet at each end, the center portion remaining fairly flat.

If you need a rocker—that is, if you do at least half your canoeing in moving water—the two models described here are great for river running. I have used them both for years and can attest to their performance in whitewater. However, the rocker that allows you to twist and turn so easily on the river becomes a barge-shaped bow on the lake that you must push through the water with each paddle stroke. I don't want to make it sound too bad, though, because in reality, the difference is not actually noticeable unless you are paddling across the lake beside another, similarly laden canoe that is better suited to that environment.

White Water: The 16-foot (5 meter) White Water was designed primarily for just good fun. It will handle two paddlers, without a significant amount of gear, on some pretty rough stretches of rapids. If your need is a solo canoe for whitewater tripping, I can think of none better suited to that purpose. It will take you and your gear over miles of whitewater river with minimum effort and insignificant splashes over the gunwale.

River Runner: The 19-foot (6-meter) River Runner is the tripping canoe for river trips or even combination trips. The nicely rockered ends allow for easy turning even when the canoe is heavily laden with gear and people, and the broad bow has a wonderful lift to it when the canoe pitches down—even when it dives into one of those dreaded foam-

River Canoes		
	White Water	**River Runner**
Length:	16' (4.8m)	19' (5.8m)
Width:	36" (1m)	39½" (1m)
Depth:	12¾" (.32m)	14" (.36m)
Stem height:	24" (.6m)	25" (.63m)
Approximate weight:	65 lbs. (30 kg)	90 lbs. (41 kg)

filled holes. Most canoes emerge from such places with at least a couple of gallons of river shifting around on the bottom, but the River Runner usually comes through high and dry.

These two canoes, like the White designs, are completely separate designs and not merely an expansion or contraction of the same canoe. If you want one or the other, you will find it much easier to use the correct plan. However, if your need is for a slightly larger or smaller version of either model, then pick the plans closest to your needs, and go for it. It will turn out fine.

19-foot River Runner. This is the 19-foot (5.8 meter) River Runner in its native environment—whitewater! The photo is of some of my students on a week-long Allagash trip. This is their first exposure to whitewater, but you wouldn't know it from the photo. They look like seasoned veterans.

Figure 2-4. Grand Laker profile.

Grand Laker

It did not take long, after the first powered canoe appeared in the Grand Lake Stream area of Maine, for folks to become aware of its advantages—especially the working guides in this popular fishing area. The first was a square stern built by the Old Town Canoe Company in 1922, but before long, square-sterned canoes were being produced locally, and the process of evolution that would eventually produce a unique canoe was under way. This model combined the needed features of the traditional canoe with those of the big, motor-powered lake boat. The result was a big canoe—certainly not of a size and shape to lend itself to paddle power, but that was able to handle a motor of up to 10 horsepower and be steady and reliable on a big lake.

At first many old-time guides would not have anything to do with the newfangled square sterns. However, to compete with the extended range of the powered canoes, guides using the traditional double-enders had to rely on the steamboat *Woodchuck* to haul their canoes up the lake in the morning and back in the evening. It was not too long before all of the guides in the area switched over. Of course, the fact that guides with powered canoes received $2 a day more than those with paddle-powered craft could have had something to do with the rapid acceptance of the canoe that was to become known as the Grand Laker.

Today, several molds exist for the Grand Lakers, and several builders make them in Maine and perhaps elsewhere. To the best of my knowledge, the builders still use the rib and plank construction. I have to confess that this canoe is the only canoe in this book of which I have no firsthand knowledge. It isn't that I have anything against motor-powered canoes; it is just that my work and pleasure do not require a canoe of this type. When I need an outboard, a motor

Grand Laker	
Length	19' 6" (6m)
Width	45" (1.1m)
Depth	18" (.5m) (center)
Stem height	26" (.7m)
Approximate weight	135 lbs. (61 kg)

bracket on my double-ender does very well; but friends and former students who do use this design tell me it does a great job, and so, on the strength of their endorsement, I offer the pattern to you.

Personal canoes

These canoes are small and light enough for one person to handle by themselves, but can support up to two people if needed.

The Wabnaki: The Wabnaki is named for our Maine and New Brunswick Native Americans—not because I claim any sort of authenticity for the shape, but because I have a strong interest in these people, and the canoe reminds me of some of their medium-sized canoes I have seen pictured. This is my favorite small canoe. It is small and light enough for one person to handle on land and on water, yet it is large enough for two people to paddle for a day out on the water. Some may wonder when I call this a small canoe, but in my opinion a canoe shorter than 16 feet (5 meters) is for a special purpose,

Personal Canoes		
	Puddle Duck	**Wabnaki**
Length	14' (4.2m)	16' (4.8m)
Width	34½" (.89m)	36" (.91m)
Depth	12" (.3m)	13" (.33m)
Height of stems	20" (.5m)	22½" (.57m)
Approximate weight	45 lbs. (20 kg)	65 lbs. (29 kg)

Wabnaki. This is the versatile Wabnaki. This is one of my three canoes of this model. I call this my show-and-tell canoe because I like to keep one canoe that looks new just to show off when the opportunity presents itself. It spends most of its time tied up in the rafters of my garage.

usually one person handling it in tight quarters. A trapper would be one good example.

I always hesitate to recommend a canoe shorter than 18 feet (5.5 meters) for an extended canoe trip. I am a "big canoe man," so to speak. However, the experienced person who wants to go it alone will not need the additional length unless he or she carries an excessive amount of gear. The word "experience" is key here. The experienced tripper knows how to pick his route on a windy day to minimize the effects of the wind and thus reach the destination for the day. By the same token, the experienced tripper knows how to load the canoe to best trim it for the current conditions. I could go on with this, but you see my point. Know your canoe and your ability.

I am fond of this little canoe; otherwise, I wouldn't have named it for a people I admire. I guess this fondness is the reason I have three of them at various locations in Maine.

The Puddle Duck: Have you ever wanted a canoe for your own private use? I don't mean the family canoe or one to use for tripping where others will be with you, but one just for you—a canoe you can leave hidden at a favorite small stream or pond

that will be there for you to use without any prior preparation. Or maybe you are a trapper or hunter or fisherman who needs to get out on small bodies of water by yourself.

The Puddle Duck is just the canoe for the situations described above. It is small and light enough for an average person to handle alone both in and out of the water. It has the capacity to carry two people, if necessary, though it is better suited to one handler and his or her tools and gear for the day's work or play.

I had my own Puddle Duck that saw service for a number of years and was hidden near the stream that borders our property. I used it on the stream during the summer months and during the fall I used it a couple of times to haul home some venison.

Of course, leaving a canoe hidden in the woods is not without risk. My little Puddle Duck was stolen from its hiding place until my best friend, Dick, came across it in his travels. The canoe was unique, so he recognized it instantly and didn't hesitate to pick it up. Later that day, I saw the little canoe coming up my driveway on top of his truck. Unfortunately, the thieves didn't take very good care of the canoe and it was damaged beyond repair.

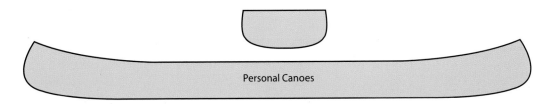

Personal Canoes

Figure 2-5. Personal Canoe profile.

The Laker

I started building canoes in the very early 1970s. At that time, I was casting about, looking for a canoe-building method that would lend itself to use by relatively unskilled high-school students with some guidance from me. A friend gave me a copy of *Popular Science* (circa 1940s) that contained an article on building a redwood canoe. That redwood canoe was what I eventually named "The Laker." (An interesting side-note; at a sportsman's show, some twenty years after the publication of the first edition of this book, a man came up to me and introduced himself as the son of the author of that article in *Popular Science*.)

I see the Laker as a canoe for casual canoeing— maybe at a summer cottage, for occasional use by family members and for youngsters to gain experience by paddling around at their leisure. The flat cross-section makes the hull stable, and the flat bottom from stem to stem almost suggests that it should have a keel. Of course, I make no bones about the fact that I believe a keel is an abomination of a canoe, but if any canoe *should* have a keel, it would be the Laker.

The Laker	
Length	16' (4.9m)
Width	36" (.9m)
Depth	13" (.33m)
Stem height	22½" (.6m)
Approximate weight	65 lbs. (29.5 kg)

(Note: May be made 13' [4m] by leaving out stations 4 & 5)

This model is unique in that its forms will build two different sizes, with no modification. From the nine stations for the 16-foot (5-meter) model, simply leave out the center station and one of its neighbors, and you have yourself a 13-footer (4-meters). (Omit stations 4 and 5, or 5 and 6.) All spacing and other measurements remain the same. This is the only canoe on which I recommend using this method to alter the length.

I have to say that the lines of this canoe do not really excite me, but it is a very practical canoe that will serve well for its intended purpose. One of my adult students used this pattern as the basis for a canoe he wanted to design himself. I was impressed with the result, so this is a possibility if you are inclined in that direction. Maybe you can design your dream canoe from this or one of the other models in the book.

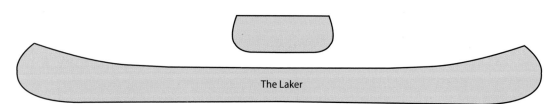

The Laker

Figure 2-6. The Laker profile.

Prepare your materials ahead of time so the building itself goes smoothly.

Chapter 3
The Preliminaries

Preparing to start a large project almost always involves a considerable amount of work that seems unproductive in itself, but is nevertheless necessary. In the case of building a strip canoe, not only are the preliminaries necessary, but also it is essential that they be done well if the finished product is to be one that you can be proud of. The strongback and the stations are nothing more than tools to be used in the construction of your canoe. As such, they will have no function once the canoe is finished any more than will your hammer and saw. However, like your other tools, their quality has much to do with the quality of your work. It is very difficult to do quality work with shoddy tools. The strips, of course, are part of the finished canoe, but are included here because sawing and machining them is a dusty job that is necessary to have behind you before the fun stuff—the building—begins.

The Strongback

The first thing you will need is a strongback: the spine that holds the stations and stem forms in place. Around this temporary frame you will build the body of your canoe. Built of 2x6s or plywood and 2x4s with some 1-inch (25mm) boards for bracing, the strongback should be long enough for the biggest canoe that you are likely to want. (You can always build a short canoe on a long strongback, but not the other way around. Take a look at **Figure 3-1**, and you will see that the strongback can be at most 2 feet (.6 meters) shorter than the canoe you will build.

Materials and tools needed to build the strongback

Materials

- Two 2x6s (or plywood) of required length
- 2x4s sufficient to make required number of 18" (457mm) crosspieces
- 1x4s sufficient to make bracing
- 2½" (64mm) drywall screws
- 1¼" (32mm) drywall screws

Tools

- Rule
- Pencil
- Handsaw or power handsaw
- Hammer
- Screwdriver or power driver
- Framing square

Top View

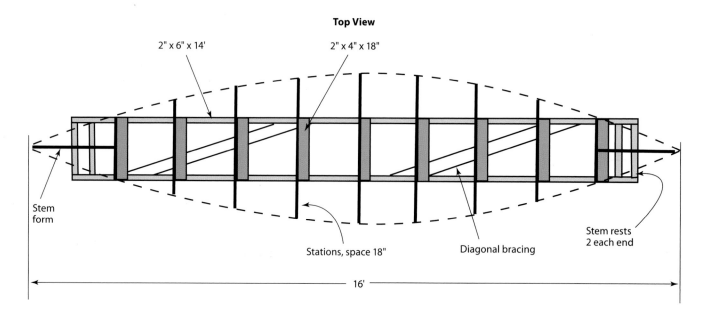

2" x 6" x 14'

2" x 4" x 18"

Stem form

Stations, space 18"

Diagonal bracing

Stem rests 2 each end

16'

Side View

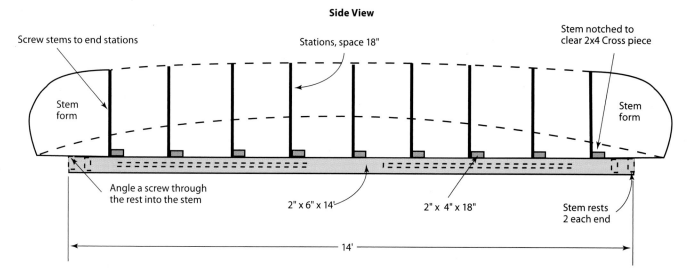

Screw stems to end stations

Stations, space 18"

Stem notched to clear 2x4 Cross piece

Stem form

Stem form

Angle a screw through the rest into the stem

2" x 6" x 14'

2" x 4" x 18"

Stem rests 2 each end

14'

Figure 3-1: Locations of the stations and the stem forms. The most common error in setting up the stations is to use the wrong side of the 2x4 crosspiece for one or more stations. Line up the stem forms exactly to the center of the first and last station.

Plywood

Through the years, it has become apparent to me that using construction grade lumber for the strongback can cause some problems because of warping and twisting of the 2x6s. It is difficult to make a canoe that is straight and true on a base that is crooked. For the strongback shown in the photo at right, I used plywood instead of 2x6s. I laminated, with glue and screws, three layers of ⅝" (16mm) CDX plywood. It turns out that using three layers is overdoing it and two layers will serve just as well. One sheet of plywood will yield eight pieces 5½" (140mm) wide, which will be enough for up to a 16-foot (4.9-meter) canoe. Cut one 5½" x 8' (140mm x 2.4m) length of plywood for each side in half to make your joints break correctly. A longer strongback will require more plywood. The plywood-based strongback will remain straight and true. It is imperative that the completed Strongback lie flat with no twist.

If you opt to use construction grade 2x6s, don't bother trying to find long ones if you are building a long canoe. Shorter pieces can be nailed or screwed together with a 3-foot (1-meter) overlap to achieve the length you require.

Multipurpose capabilities

If you look closely at the strongback in the photo above right, you will notice that it has 2x4s on both sides. On one side, the 2x4s are spaced 18" (457mm) apart, and on the other side, they are spaced 20" (508mm) apart. This allows me to make any canoe in the book on the same strongback. Not visible in the photo is the fact that the strongback is made in two parts. The part in the foreground will build a canoe up to 16 feet (4.9 meters) long. By bolting on the extension, as I did for the canoe we will be building in this book, I am able to build up to a 20-foot (6-meter) canoe. Workshop space being what it is for most of us, this also allows me to build a shorter canoe without dealing with several feet of unnecessary strongback.

Some canoes, the 14-foot (4.3-meter) Puddle Duck and the 20-foot (6.1-meter) White Guide Model for example, require a 20-inch (508mm) spacing of the stations. You can use the other side of the strongback for this purpose as discussed. This way

The strongback is the foundation of your canoe. It is a temporary foundation, but is every bit as important as the permanent foundation of a building. Keep it straight and true. Consider using plywood instead of construction grade 2x6s.

you will not have to disturb the 18-inch (457mm) spacing, which you may want to use in the future.

It is a good idea to assemble the strongback with inexpensive drywall screws so that changes are easily made when needed. (By the way, this two-sided strongback is the reason we attached those braces to cleats on the inside of the strongback instead of to the bottom.) If you use a long strongback for a shorter canoe, you will have to remove one of the 2x4s to make room for the stem form. Then attach a couple of cross pieces flush with the top of the 2x6s for the stem form to rest on. The stem forms are screwed to the two end stations and a screw angled up through the bottom of the stem rest will hold it securely.

Spacing the stations

Cut enough 18-inch (457mm) lengths of 2x4 for the number of stations—forms—you plan to have. The usual spacing is 18 or 20 inches (457 or 508mm), but this can be adjusted within reason toward any final length. Be sure to space the 2x4s from the same side each time and to screw the stations to that side. Find the pattern for the stations of the canoe you are building inside the back cover.

Look at Figure 3-1; it shows the correct layout and spacing for a 16-foot (4.9-meter) canoe. With stations 18 inches (457mm) apart, note that the end of the stem forms will be 24 inches (610mm) from stations 1 and 9. Fourteen-foot (4.3-meter) 2x6s will be long enough to build a 16-foot (4.9-meter) canoe. Put in two or three diagonal braces, as shown in Figure 3-1, to help make the strongback more rigid; screw these braces to cleats inside the 2x6s.

Shortening a design: There are two ways to shorten or lengthen a canoe design. The first is to add or remove stations. The Laker is the only canoe in the book that this method is recommended for. In most cases, this kind of shortening results in the need to make some adjustments to the stations to ensure a smooth hull without waves or bumps. Once they have been altered for the new length, the stations are unfit for their original purpose.

A more practical method of shortening or lengthening is to change the spacing of the stations. For example, suppose you like the looks of the 16-foot (4.9-meter) Wabnaki, but would like a 17-foot (5.2-meter) canoe. By increasing the spacing of the stations by only 1½ inches (38mm), to 19½" (495mm) instead of 18" (457mm), you will add the extra foot (305mm) in length without changing the lines of the canoe. I do not recommend changing the spacing by more than 2 or 2½ inches (51 or 64mm), but if you feel the need, go ahead and experiment a little. Tack on some trial strips before you start stripping to ensure the result will please you.

Your strongback will last indefinitely if you take care of it. Keep it out of the weather and be sure to store it lying flat so it will not twist.

Pattern Note

Including full-size station patterns for all eight canoes required printing on both sides of the paper. To use a pattern without destroying the one on the reverse side of the paper, simply use carbon or graphite paper to copy it to a different large sheet of paper. (Graphite paper is less messy and available in larger sizes than carbon paper.) The centerline and the bottom line of the stations are common to all of the patterns; to prevent wear on the original, just make a tick mark on both ends of the straight lines and then connect the tick marks with a straightedge on the finished copy of the pattern. Each station pattern except the center one makes two stations; they should be marked as such.

The Stations

The stations, or forms, give your canoe its shape. A sloppy job of making them will cause all manner of problems later on, so trace your pattern accurately. Use a framing square lined up with the edge of your half pattern to draw the centerline of each station, instead of just depending on the edge of the paper pattern. Be sure each centerline is square with the bottom edge of the station. Keep these centerlines clearly visible on the finished stations; they are handy later on.

Except for the center one, each station has a twin on the other end of the canoe, and each pattern represents one half of a station. There are exceptions; sometimes canoes are built with the stern a littler fuller than the bow. This means that the stern would look something like the freighter-shaped canoe in Figure 2-1 on page 13, while the bow would be more like the streamlined one. This has some advantage when operating in shallow water. When a motor is mounted at the stern, the fullness gives a little extra flotation to support the additional weight. None of the patterns in this book are of this type, however. Another exception is the Grand Laker: each of its stations is unique.

The stations are made of ½" or ⅝" (13mm or 16mm) plywood. Buy CDX plywood (sheathing); this will be the least expensive. I have tried the material sold under the trade name of Aspenite (and probably others), which is a sheathing made up of wood flakes and small chips bonded together. It is less expensive than CDX plywood, but was not satisfactory, as the staples could not hold in it. You will need two sheets for a 9- or 11-station canoe. Lay out your patterns carefully and plan so as to have

Materials and tools needed to build the stations

Materials	Tools
■ 2 sheets of ½" or ⅝" (13mm or 16mm) CDX plywood	■ Framing square
	■ Pencil
	■ Band saw or saber saw
	■ Paper patterns
	■ Coarse wood rasp or power rotary grinder

the least amount of waste; then, cut the stations out with a portable jig saw or a band saw.

For later convenience, you should number your stations and mark them as to the size and type of canoe they are designed to build. If you build canoes of other shapes and sizes later on, you will be glad you did. Also, it never hurts to have your name on them in case you loan them out.

The stations can be re-used for a long time. I have never kept track of how many canoes a set will build, but I know it is a considerable number. They do get kind of ragged on the edge after a gazillion staples and screws have been in and out of them, especially on the edges where screws are needed. If your stations get ragged with use, just mix up some epoxy with cotton fibers (you will read how to mix this stuff later on; see page 38) and apply it to the damaged edges of the stations. When cured, the epoxy will hold the staples better then the original plywood edges. Keep in mind, unless you build a lot of canoes, none of this maintenance will be necessary.

Stem forms

Once you have the stations done, you have to make the stem forms. Make these by laminating two layers of the same ½" or ⅝" (13mm or 16mm) plywood, thus making the stems twice as thick as the stations. If you are running short of plywood, simply make one complete stem and then laminate on pieces left over from your cutting. The extra thickness of the stems is needed for strength and substance when the strips are attached to them.

Once you have your stem forms cut out, the curved edge has to be brought to a point. **Figure 3-2** shows this in cross section. You will have to estimate the angle for this, but it is not too critical—it would take a gross error to affect the shape of the canoe. A coarse rasp or a rotary grinder with coarse paper will do a good job of removing the wood to get the desired result. **Figure 3-3** will give you an idea of the areas to remove. The top area of the stem is rounded over. You will need to cut away a slot in the bottom of at least one of the stems to clear the 2x4 crosspiece.

Before we leave this matter of stems, I want to take this opportunity to settle something that has been a

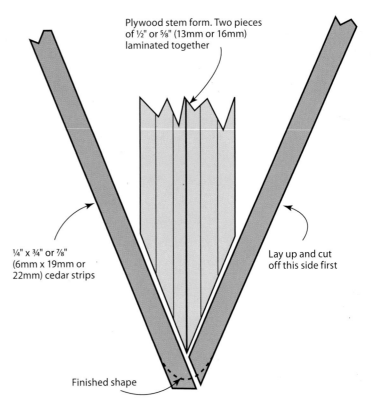

Plywood stem form. Two pieces of ½" or ⅝" (13mm or 16mm) laminated together

¼" x ¾" or ⅞" (6mm x 19mm or 22mm) cedar strips

Lay up and cut off this side first

Finished shape

Figure 3-2: Fitting strips to stem form. This drawing shows the correct fitting of the strips to the shaped stem form. The angle cut can be made on either side, but line your saw up carefully with the end station.

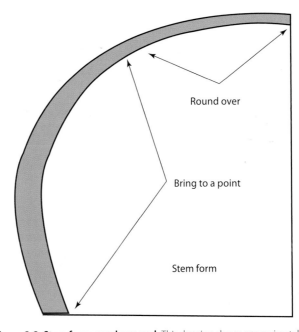

Round over

Bring to a point

Stem form

Figure 3-3: Stem form wood removal. This drawing shows approximately where to remove wood to achieve the "point" needed to attach the strips to the stem form. The exact angle is not important, as long as you have it so there is a good surface to attach the strips.

thorn in my side for nearly 30 years—ever since the original *Building a Strip Canoe*, the first edition, was in print. During that time, the book was updated as needed, but basically remained as I had originally written it. In those years it was the subject of several reviews by "experts" of unknown (to me at least) qualifications. Most comments were positive, but the one negative was that I didn't use hardwood stems.

Until now, I never had the chance to defend my choice of not using hardwood stems. The reason I don't use them is that they are totally unnecessary, and represent a lot of careful fitting for zero benefit. In more than 30 years of guiding wilderness canoe trips on Maine's white water rivers, I had occasion to make many and varied repairs to my strip canoes. Never did I have to make repairs to the bow or stern. However, the most convincing incident to support my position happened on dry land.

We had just finished a strip canoe in my shop at school. I had agreed to take it to the owner. At the end of class, I was busy and had some students take the canoe outside and tie it down on top of my truck, thinking that I would check their work before I left for the day. I forgot to check and headed for home. It was a windy day, and about halfway home a gust of wind caused the canoe to slide sideways and lift off my truck. I remember seeing clearly, in my rear-view mirror, the canoe tumbling end-over-end on the pavement behind me. I felt sick to my stomach, but there was nothing to do but load the canoe and get home. The only damage was a thwart and seat torn loose, and some cosmetic damage to one of the stems—it looked as if someone had taken a coarse rasp to it.

So, go ahead and put in hardwood stem pieces if you wish, but your canoe will be plenty strong without them!

The Strips

The strips are what will show on the outside of your canoe. There are many types of wood you could select to serve as the strips, but the important things to consider are weight and flexibility. You don't want to worry about lugging a heavy canoe around, nor do you want to think too much about bending the strips to fit the canoe.

Wood choices

The choice of wood from which to make the strips depends upon where you live. Most often, a wood native to your area will be less expensive than a wood imported from some other part of the country. However, deals do come along. Even though I live about as far from California as one can get, I have built canoes of redwood. You have a wide choice, but keep weight in mind as you make that choice.

I have made canoes of five different woods: redwood, Western red cedar, Northern white cedar, white pine, and basswood. The last three are native to my area. Of the five, I prefer the cedars above the others and the white cedar is my favorite of these. It is lightweight; the lightest of the woods named here, I believe. It is limber; it bends easily during construction with no special preparation. And, white cedar has a pleasing variety of colors when finished naturally, ranging from almost white to a rich honey color.

Redwood, besides being expensive, is rather brittle and breaks easily during construction. I often found it necessary to soak the redwood strips for a few minutes to combat breakage.

Pine bends well, but is heavier than cedar and offers no advantage that I can see, except perhaps easy availability.

Basswood is a much-overlooked wood these days. Years ago, woodworkers relied upon it for a variety of uses because it was easily available. The only fault I can find with basswood for strip-canoe building is that it is heavier than cedar, and the grain and coloration are not very attractive or pleasing to the eye in the finished strip canoe.

Length of wood

A lot of builders have contacted me to ask where they can get cedar long enough to build a canoe. Don't worry about it—you can use as many pieces of strips as is necessary to achieve your length. The joints do not weaken the canoe at all! Northern white cedar trees taper sharply as they grow. This means that getting long boards is not economical. One year I couldn't find any quality cedar except from a cedar fence manufacturer. It was all four feet (1.2 meters) long. We made a lot of joints that year, but the canoes were just as strong and attractive as any others. Joint-making is covered later (see page 32). The joints do not have to be made on the stations (they won't be there when the canoe is done anyway, remember?) Securing the joints is covered in the building chapter (page 29). Just remember to break your joints—don't let them fall along the same vertical line, or there will look like there is a seam in the finished canoe. Use random lengths to prevent this.

Purchasing the wood

In the Appendix, I have listed some sources of supplies and materials, including wood, but I strongly urge you to thoroughly exhaust all possible local sources before ordering from an outside source.

The following figures are for the building of the 18.5 foot (5.6 meter) White Guide Model that was used to illustrate this book. The quantities are meant

Materials and tools needed to make the strips

Materials	Tools
■ 75 board feet (More or less, see text) of ¾" or ⅞" (19mm or 22mm) boards (wood of your choice)	■ Rule ■ Table saw with sharp blade ■ Router or shaper (optional) ■ Push stick ■ Dust mask ■ Safety glasses

only as a guide for you to determine the amount you may need for your canoe. We started with 71 board feet of white cedar lumber. This yielded 1936 linear feet (590 linear meters) of strips. We had 73 linear feet (22 linear meters) left over, so we actually used 62 board feet of cedar lumber, and a total of 1863 linear feet (568 linear feet) of strips. So plan on 70 to 75 board feet of lumber to build the 18.5-foot (5.6 meter) White Guide canoe.

Unless you have a surface planer, you should buy the boards finished to ¾" or ⅞" (19mm or 22mm) thickness. A uniform thickness is very important because it determines the width of your strips. Most of the time I go with the thicker ⅞" (22mm) boards if possible. Once you have your lumber to a uniform thickness, you are ready to start stripping on the table saw. Cut the strips ¼" (6mm) thick. Again, uniformity is important, and so is safety. This is a boring job, so pay attention and take a break if you find your mind wandering.

Cutting strips. To do a good job of laying up strips for your canoe, it is essential that the strips be of uniform width and thickness. The width (a product of the board thickness) is especially important because you will be joining strips end-to-end.

Bead and cove

Machining a bead and cove on your strips is not an absolute necessity, but it really makes for a much better-looking hull and will cut your need for filling by 90% or more. The photo at right shows the advantage of using the bead and cove as opposed to just leaving the edges square. A source for router bits to make the bead and cove can be found in the Appendix (page 109). The photo below shows a setup to run the strips through with uniform results. The setup shown is on a shaper, but the same thing would work with a table-mounted router. The fingers that hold the strip down and firmly against the fence are easily made with thin strips of hardwood, 1⁄16" to 1⁄8" (2mm to 3mm) thick. Glue them to a slot in scrap wood as shown in the photo.

Route the bead side first, because the edges of the cove are delicate and easily damaged. Adjusting the router/shaper takes a little time to get right because you are working with such thin material, but once you have it with the setup shown, you can go through your entire pile of strips and know that they are uniform.

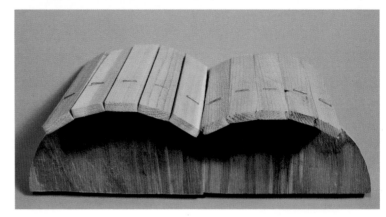

Bead and cove. This photo shows the importance of the bead and cove. You can build a perfectly serviceable canoe with square-edge strips, but for a really good job, take the time to do the bead and cove.

Bead and cove router set-up. This is an easily made set-up for producing uniform results with the bead and cove bits. The hardwood fingers are 1⁄16" to 1⁄8" (2mm to 3mm) thick and are glued in the slot in the holders. The set-up shown here is on a shaper, but the same will work for a table-mounted router.

Building the hull is the first step to constructing your canoe.

Chapter 4

Building the Hull

Now that you have those boring (but important) preliminaries over with, it is time to start putting things together and watch your canoe take shape. To me, this is the most exciting part of building a canoe—watching it grow into a beautiful, sleek, yet extremely functional form. It is the same whether it is a model that I have built many times before, or a new design that I am trying for the first time. After watching over 500 of them take shape, I still thrill to see it.

Materials and tools needed to build the hull

Materials

- Strongback
- 1 set of plywood stations
- 1¼" (32mm) drywall screws
- Small nails (a few)
- Piece or pieces of strapping (canoe length)
- Masking tape
- Cedar strips sufficient for the size canoe to be built
- 2 or 3 containers of carpenter's glue
- 2 or 3 boxes of ⁹⁄₁₆" (14mm) staples
- 60- and 80-grit sandpaper for sanders
- Epoxy resin and hardener (small amount)
- Silica
- Cedar flour
- Latex gloves
- Dust masks

Tools

- Tacker capable of driving ⁹⁄₁₆" (14mm) staples
- Hammer
- Handsaw (fine-toothed)
- Block plane
- Chalkline, 3 or 4 feet (1 meter) longer than the canoe
- 2 sawhorses
- 3 or 4 C-clamps
- Tack puller or similar tool to pull staples
- Paint scraper(s)
- Surform plane or fine rasp
- Putty knife
- Power sander (Random orbit recommended)
- Extra hands if available

Laying Up the Strips

3

Establish the center line. Jason carefully aligns the stations using a taut line stretched from the centers of the first and last stations. This prevents misalignment of the stations due to a possible misalignment of the strongback. Once all the stations are in place, the stem pieces are centered on the first and last stations and secured with drywall screws.

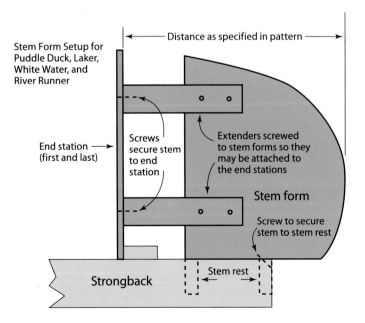

Stem Form Setup for Puddle Duck, Laker, White Water, and River Runner

← Distance as specified in pattern →

End station (first and last)

Screws secure stem to end station

Extenders screwed to stem forms so they may be attached to the end stations

Stem form

Screw to secure stem to stem rest

Stem rest

Strongback

Figure 4-1: Stem form set-up for the Puddle Duck, Laker, White Water, and River Runner. A good alternative to this would be to extend the stems the required distance when making them from the patterns. This way the stems could be secured directly to the first and last station.

1. Position the strongback.
Start by setting up the strongback on a couple of sawhorses to raise it to a convenient height.

2. Mount the end stations.
Next, take the first and last station and mount them in their proper places at each end of the strongback. Be sure they are centered on the 2x4 crosspieces, and the bottoms of the stations align with the bottoms of the crosspieces.

3. Establish the center line.
Now drive a small nail in the top center of the two end stations, and stretch a line tautly between them. You can get the line tighter if you anchor it to the ends of the strongback. All of the remaining stations are centered on this taut line, not on the strongback. The use of the line ensures that the canoe will be straight, even though the strongback may be slightly off.

4. Attach the other stations.
Use drywall screws to secure the stations to the strongback so they can be easily released when the time comes.

5. Mount the stem forms.
Now, with all the stations in place, take the stem forms and mount them in the center of the strongback and at the proper distance from the first and last station. If you are building one of the White models, the Wabnaki, or the Grand Laker, the stem forms are made to the correct length, so they may be butted directly against the first and last station and screwed to them. For the other models, screw on extenders as shown in **Figure 4-1** and mount them the same way. Otherwise, you could extend the stem forms to the required length when making them from the patterns. Also shown in Figure 4-1 is a screw angled up through the stem rest into the stem. This makes it easy to release the stems when the time comes, yet holds them securely.

6. Tape over the edges.

Use masking tape to cover the edges of the plywood stations and the stem forms. This is to prevent gluing the strips to the stations, making it easy to remove the hull when it is time. Be sure to apply a wide band of tape to each side of the stem form where the strips will touch it.

7. Nail on the temporary support.

Next, take a piece (or pieces) of scrap wood or strapping and lay it down the center of the stations. Make sure each station is vertical and put a small nail through the wood into the station. This is just a temporary thing to keep the stations stationary and vertical while you start laying on the strips. After a few strips are in place, this temporary support may be removed.

8. Eyeball the whole thing.

All should look straight and symmetrical. Usually a critical eye can spot any error that has been made at this point. If everything looks well aligned, you are ready to start putting on the strips.

Tape over the edges. Kelly is applying masking tape to the edges of the stations and the stem pieces to ensure an easy release of the canoe from the stations when the time comes. Clear packaging tape could be used as well. Be sure to tape a wide band on both sides of the stem pieces.

Nail on the temporary support. To be sure that the stations stand vertical and do not shift when you start laying on strips, secure them with temporary scrap pieces like these. Use a small nail. Once a few strips are in place, the temporary pieces may be removed.

Grand Laker stern

If you are building a Grand Laker, everything will be set up about the same as shown, except that the square stern is to be a permanent part of the finished hull. Make the stern piece from 1½" (38mm) oak, ash, or other strong hardwood. It is okay to glue up pieces with waterproof glue (use your epoxy for this) to obtain the required width. Place the stern at 10 degrees from vertical, with the top (as it sits on the strongback, actually the bottom of the canoe) leaning toward the bow. See **Figure 4-2**. The stern is held in place at the proper height by a piece of plywood, as indicated in the plans. Once the stern is positioned and held at the proper angle you should relieve the edge, as indicated in Figure 4-2, so that it will receive the strips flush without leaving a gap on the inside.

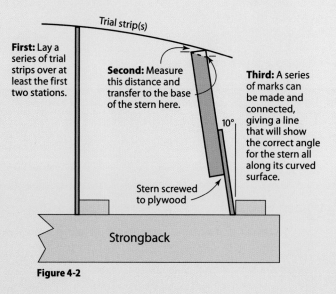

Trial strip(s)

First: Lay a series of trial strips over at least the first two stations.

Second: Measure this distance and transfer to the base of the stern here.

Third: A series of marks can be made and connected, giving a line that will show the correct angle for the stern all along its curved surface.

10°

Stern screwed to plywood

Strongback

Figure 4-2

Laying Up the Strips (continued)

9

Attach the first strip. Before mounting this first sheer strip, glue up the joints so as to make one continuous strip. This ensures a smooth lay of the as-yet-unsupported strip. This is the only time pre-joining is done. Once the sheer strip is in place, give it a good look-over to be sure you have a smooth and fair shape. If there is a problem with the stations, this is the time to take care of it.

9. Attach the first strip.

The first strip establishes the sheer of the canoe. Some strip builders run the first strip straight out to the stem form and then fill in the remaining areas below (actually above on the finished canoe) with short pieces. I think it looks best to have the strips follow the canoe's sheer line if possible and practical. An exception is on the Grand Laker: the up-turn at the bow is so sharp on that canoe that the wood will refuse to bend without breaking.

For the first strip, and only the first strip, I prefer to glue the pieces of strip together ahead of time so as to make one continuous strip to establish the sheer line. This ensures a smooth line. Also, it is a good idea to use a drywall screw in each station of the sheer line strip to ensure a solid base to continue stripping.

10. Examine your work so far.

When the sheer line strip is on both sides, walk around and look it over. It should be a clean and symmetrical line from one end to the other. Sometimes a small error in making the stations will show up here and must be corrected by removing some wood from the station(s) or adding a little to make the correction. I have added wood for this by taking pieces of scrap cedar strips and stapling them to the stations to bring the line to where it should be.

11. Avoid lining up the joints.

The ends of your strips can be joined anywhere they fall; they do not have to be made on a station. However, it is important that you break your joints randomly. This avoids lining the joints up and forming what appears to be a seam in the canoe. You will, without a doubt, have many strips of equal length, so you have to consciously work to avoid having joints line up with each other. When making the angle shown in the photo at left, just be sure to have the cove side of the strip up every time.

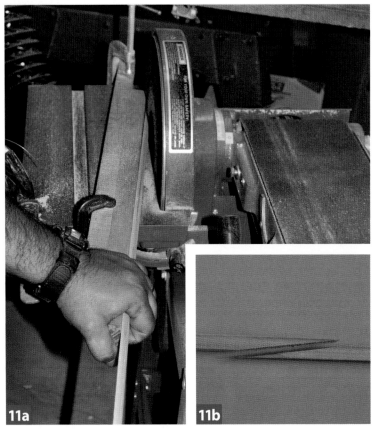

11a **11b**

Avoid lining up the joints. Make the long tapered joint seen here with the disc sander setup shown. Keep the same side (cove side recommended) up each time you shape the end. The actual angle used isn't important, as long as it is the same for each of the mated pieces.

12a

Run glue on the strip edges. The bead of glue does not have to be large to secure the strips. Do not give in to the temptation to wipe off the excess glue as you go along. This will only rub the glue into the grain of the wood, making it difficult to get off later. It is much easier to remove the glue in lumps.

12b

Clamp the strips. These Erwin clamps work great for securing the tapered joints while the glue dries. Continue to lay strips by running the next strip through the jaws of the clamp. By the time you lay two additional strips, the joint will have dried enough to remove the clamp.

12c

Staple the strips. Each time you drive a staple, be sure that the bead of the new strip is firmly squeezed into the cove of the strip below. While this seems to be a "duh," it isn't. If you don't pay close attention, the strip can hang up on the edge of the cove and the glue will hide the error. You will not discover it until it is too late to correct.

12. Staple the strips in place.

When you are satisfied with the first strip, lay a bead of glue on the upper edge. If you cut beads and coves, you will be putting the glue into the cove. Staple the strips in place with 9⁄16" (14mm) staples in each station. Put one or two staples between the stations to keep the strips aligned with each other. Since the end of the strips bend downward, it is a good idea to put a drywall screw through each strip into the stem piece. Other than that, use drywall screws only where the staple will not do the job. As you work your way upward over the stations, the screws help keep the strip from lifting. Make every strip lay as flat as possible. In short, do what you have to do to make the strips behave as you wish them to behave.

12d

Apply screws at the stem. Secure each strip with a screw at the stem. Because the strips make an edge bend at this point, it is common for the strip to lift a little, leaving a small gap between the strips.

12e

Keep the strips flat. When you start laying strips over the curved part of the station, the strip will tend to lift on the upper edge. (It tries to keep going up straight.) Be diligent in keeping the strips as flat against the curved form as possible. It will be necessary to use screws in most cases.

Laying Up the Strips (continued)

13

Cut the strips at the stem. Cut the strips from the first side at an angle, as shown. Do this by lining your saw up with the first station or the strips below. You will scrape off some of the tape from the stem, so replace it as needed. Don't try to lay up too many strips before cutting. Five or six is usually the maximum, and as you get closer to the top of the stem, do even fewer. When you start to strip the other side, the strips will be laid past the ones you cut at an angle, and cut off square.

14a

Glue the strips at the stem. When both sides are even, work some glue between the strips at the angle cut and clamp the two sides together. The blocks of wood shown are cut at a slight angle to prevent the clamp from sliding off. Keep the wood blocks slightly below the top of the top strip so you can continue laying strips. By the time you have completed another five or six, the lower one will be dry and you can remove the clamp.

13. Avoid twisting the strips.

Symmetrically, lay up about five or six strips on one side and trim the ends as shown in the photo at left; then, switch to the other side. Sometimes, if the canoe has a severe upturn near the end, the first few strips will tend to twist due to the severe edgewise bend. If this happens, use a C-clamp and a couple of pieces of scrap wood to hold them in place until the glue dries. If you lay up the same side first every time, all your cuts will be on the same side. This is not important, however.

14. Glue the angled end strips together.

Once you have the two sides equal, it is a good idea to work some glue between the angle cut and the opposing strip and clamp the ends together. Use some scrap wood cut at the correct angle so the clamp will bring the ends in without slipping off. See photo at bottom left.

14b

Lower the canoe if needed. The canoe is about half stripped here. At this point, depending on the height of the builders, you may want to lower the canoe to make things more accessible. In our case here, we simply laid the sawhorses on their side and rested the strongback on the braces.

15. Lay strips over the stem form.

The most difficult area in laying strips is when you bring them up and over the stem form. Within a few strips, you are making the transition from a primarily vertical lay to a horizontal one. Here, you use your best judgment. It seems every canoe I have done was a little different in this area, even on the same set of forms. I have no explanation for this, only to say do what you have to do. One thing you can do ahead of time is to round over the stem form at the top, and if it seems necessary, take more of the stem off at the top as you approach it with your strips if it helps bring things together.

16. Fit the ends of the strips as you go.

Once you have completed the transition from vertical to horizontal, start alternating strips from one side to the other, fitting the ends as you go along. This gives a nice-looking seam down the keel line of the canoe, as you can see in the photos. In fitting these bottom strips, it is easiest to make an angle fit on each end and then fit a strip in between. This avoids having to make the angle and make it exactly the right length. The in-between strip is easier to fit to the proper length.

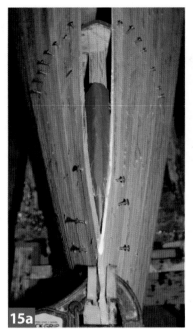

15a

15b

Lay strips over the stem form. Here we have reached the most difficult spot in laying up the strips. In just a couple of strips, we go from what is essentially a vertical lay to a horizontal lay. Before this photo was taken, I took some more wood off the rounded top of the stem piece to make the strips lay a little better. You can see where my rasp slipped and gouged the left hand strip. Fortunately, the damage was not serious enough to require replacement.

Make the transition. Here we have accomplished the transition from vertical to horizontal with two strips. Lay the first strip (the one on the right) as is and extend it over the end of the canoe. Carefully carve the next strip until it fits into the long tapered opening.

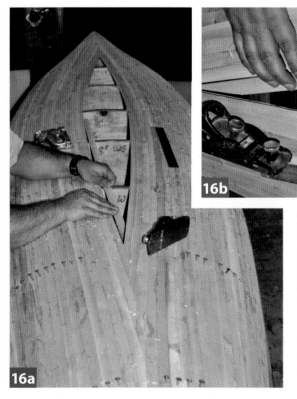

16a

16b

Alternate from one side to the other as you lay strips on the bottom. Carefully fit each strip into the facing one. Once the angle is correct, round it off a little with a block plane so it will fit into the cove of the facing strip.

16c

Fit the ends as you go. The best way to complete the bottom is by using three pieces of strip for each side. Fit the two ends where an angle is required, then fit a piece in between the two. This is much easier than trying to get the correct angle and the correct length.

Laying Up the Strips (continued)

17

Pull the staples.
This staple puller is a modified tack puller. Just screw on a short length of dowel to make a fulcrum to pry out the staple. A variety of tools will work for staple pulling. Just use something that doesn't make too much of a dent or dig in the soft cedar.

17. Let dry and pull the staples.

When the strips are all laid up and the glue is dry, it is staple-pulling time! A small tack puller, available from hardware stores, will do a good job of this. A screwdriver will work, and it will work even better if modified by grinding the end to a sharp edge. Any tool you can find that will get under those staples and lift them out will do the job. You can also remove all of the drywall screws used to hold things in place. They are saved to use another day. Once all the hardware has been removed and nothing but glue is holding things together, you are ready for the smoothing operation.

Smoothing Up

Finally, you can see the shape of your canoe! It is like a gem in the rough, but still, the beauty is there. As you work now, the beauty will deepen until the final steps when the canoe is ready to launch. The smoothing is another of those boring, but necessary, jobs. At the same time, it is exciting because it is here that you bring the canoe from its rough state to a beautiful smooth shape.

1. Smooth the bow and stern.

The ends, both bow and stern, have to be smoothed up. Do this with a Surform plane or a fine rasp. Make a smooth rounded profile by standing back and eyeballing it, making corrections until it satisfies your eye. When the profile is to your satisfaction, round over the end as shown in Figure 3-2. This round over is important, because fiberglass will not lie well on a sharp point.

2. Scrape off the excess glue.

The next smoothing step is to scrape off the excess glue. Ordinary paint scrapers work well for this. The photo below shows how to modify the scraper blades for this work. One blade is rounded to do the inside of the canoe. The other blade is straight, but the corners are rounded off to prevent accidental gouging with the sharp corner of the original blade. Once the blades are ground to shape, simply file a new cutting edge.

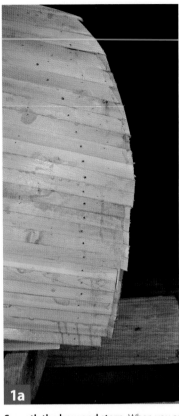

Smooth the bow and stern. When you are finished laying up your strips, the ends will look ragged (photo above left). Using a Surform plane or a fine rasp, smooth out the ends so you have a nice smooth line. Before you are finished smoothing up the hull, you will round off the ends as shown in Figure 3-2 on page 25.

Scrape off the excess glue. Scraping off the glue is important, because if gobs of dried glue are left, they will clog the sandpaper and require frequent paper changes.

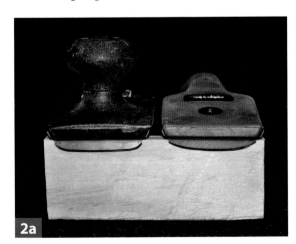

Modify the paint scrapers. The scraper blade on the left is modified on the ends to ensure that no sharp points dig into the wood. The blade on the right is rounded to facilitate scraping the glue from the inside of the hull later. After altering the blades, simply re-sharpen with a file.

Smoothing Up (continued)

3a

Sand the hull. Here, Jason is starting to smooth up the hull. Those aggressive random orbit sanders make relatively short work of this job, although sanding is never a favorite pastime for any woodworker.

3b

Lay the canoe on its side if needed. Your best work is done when you are comfortable. Laying the canoe on its side made Kelly's job of sanding the sides a little less tiring. The canoe sanding is nearly complete until after the filling is cured and ready to be sanded smooth.

4

Fill the screw holes. Use a mixture of epoxy-hardener thickened with silica and cedar flour. The dark color on the surface will not show after sanding even if you leave some of it there, because the first step in fiberglassing is a sealer coating that contains the same stuff.

3. Sand the hull.

After the glue has been scraped, the hull needs to be sanded. The sanding is easiest with a random orbit sander, as shown. With 60-grit paper, the random orbit sander makes short work of the job, and does it well. It is a dusty job, so be sure to wear a dust mask. Be sure to get all of the glue off the surface of the strips that you may have missed in the scraping process—it will show up later if you don't. At this point, there is no reason to sand with a finer paper; the scratches left with 60 grit will not show after fiberglassing. However, if you wish, you can continue with 80-grit paper. Save the sanding dust you collect in the sander's dust bag. I call this cedar flour, and you will use it later.

4. Fill any holes.

When you have the hull sanded to your satisfaction, it is time to fill any holes that may exist. These will include the screw holes, but there may also be small knotholes, chips, gaps, and cracks. The best filler for this purpose is a mixture of epoxy, thickened with silica and cedar flour. Thoroughly mix a small amount of epoxy resin with the recommended amount of hardener. Thicken the epoxy mixture with the silica and cedar flour until you have a peanut butter-like consistency and scrape the mixture into the holes. The cedar flour will make the mixture darker than your cedar strips, but during fiberglassing the strips will darken and your fills will be nearly invisible. Don't worry about filling the staple holes—they will be filled with the sealer coat in the fiberglassing phase of your building.

5. Sand the cured filler.

When the filler has cured, at least 24 hours later, sand each filled spot until the area around the fill is smooth, and the only filler visible is in the hole. A little on the surface will not show after the surface is sealed in the fiberglassing phase. When sanding the filled areas, do a generalized sanding of the area. Do not concentrate the sanding on the small area of the fill—if you do, you will cause a shallow depression that may be visible when the canoe is finished and is nice and shiny.

That's it for the hull-building phase. You are ready to move on to the fiberglassing phase.

Chapter 5

Fiberglassing

The fiberglassing portion of the strip canoe building process is, for most people, scary and intimidating. There is good reason: the stuff is expensive, and delving into the unknown with so much expensive material at stake will cause anyone to worry. And it isn't just the expense either: making a serious mistake here could ruin everything that was done previously. Not to worry. Between the information in this chapter and the epoxy manufacturer's instructions, you have the information you need to succeed.

Materials and tools needed to fiberglass the canoe hull

Materials

- Fiberglass fabric, 6-ounce, 60" (1524mm) wide; enough to cover the canoe with the desired number of layers (Add a yard or so extra)
- Epoxy and hardener sufficient for the canoe to be built (see text)
- Minimum order of silica for thickening
- Minimum order of cotton fibers for making waterproof glue
- Clean sticks to mix resin
- Plastic to cover floor
- 12 (or more) pairs of disposable gloves
- 6 disposable brushes, 2" (51mm)
- Cedar flour

Tools

- Scissors
- Old clothes
- 2 Roller pans
- 2 Roller frames
- 12 Roller covers
- 4 Squeegees
- Sander (random orbit recommended)
- Sanding discs, 60, 80, and 120 grit

Optional Tools

- Resin and hardener pumps
- 6 34-ounce mixing pots
- Goggles
- Dust masks

About Fiberglassing

My building experience with epoxy has been with two suppliers: WEST System products, supplied by Gougeon Brothers of Bay City, Michigan; and RAKA, of Fort Pierce, Florida. There are other suppliers, but I have not used them, and so will not comment on them. You will find both of these supply sources in the Appendix (page 109). I can find no difference between the two except for the mixing ratio of the epoxy and hardener. Wherever you buy your epoxy, follow the mixing directions and the safety instructions of the supplier.

It is important that you read and follow the manufacturer's instructions before starting your fiberglassing project. This chapter is designed to give you an overview of the process, but there is no way that a book such as this could stay current with changes that a manufacturer might make. Be especially attentive to mixing instructions because the ratio of hardener to resin is critical. Get it right! Also, it is important to note that a supplier may offer more than one product, each of which is mixed at a different ratio. You may note some variation in application techniques between my instructions here and the manufacturer's recommendations. What I describe are methods that have evolved in nearly 40 years of building more than 500 strip canoes and have worked well for this particular application. Gougeon Brothers, who supply WEST System products, are in the business of building sailboats and so their techniques have been developed for that application. Read theirs and mine and you be the judge.

The proper environment for fiberglassing

The environment where you do the fiberglassing will have a bearing on your success. You need a warm place: 70–75° F (21–24° C) is best, without too much humidity. High humidity turns the finished product a milky white, which is very unattractive for a strip canoe. Be aware that where you store the fiberglass cloth could cause humidity problems too. If the cloth is stored in an area of high humidity and then brought in and applied to the canoe right away, you could have the same problem described above. Allow the cloth to normalize with the air in the shop before using it.

Note on polyester resin

In the very earliest version of *Building a Strip Canoe*, I included information in this chapter on the use of polyester resins. In the very early years, I used the polyester resin in my shop for the canoes we built. It didn't take long to discover that the canoes we turned out did not last very long. The fiberglass started to separate from the wood, and very soon a general deterioration took place. Over the years I have corresponded and talked to some builders who used this resin to save money. None I have talked to were satisfied with the result. For these reasons, I have dropped all instructions for its use. If you insist on using polyester resin for your canoe project, you should be able to obtain instructions from the seller. Be sure to get complete safety instructions as well—the fumes from that stuff are really bad news. A very well-ventilated work area is mandatory!

Tools and Materials

You should be able to buy all of your tools and materials from one source. Both WEST System and RAKA have a complete catalog of materials, far beyond what you will need for fiberglassing a canoe. Both catalogs are on the Internet, and WEST System has dealers throughout the country. Some dealers, however, carry only a limited inventory.

Fiberglass cloth

The fiberglass cloth you use will have a major effect on the final weight of your canoe. The material is sold in ounces per yard, and the heavier cloth you use, the more the canoe will weigh. The heavier cloth not only adds weight by itself, but it will hold more resin, resulting in even more pounds. Unless you have special reasons to do otherwise, keep your life simple as possible by buying only one weight and doubling up where extra strength is needed. Six-ounce cloth is the best choice for strip canoe building purposes, and cloth 60" (1.5m) wide will be needed for most canoes. If you plan to put on a football-shaped piece to double up the bottom of your canoe, you can buy a narrow fiberglass cloth for that—36" and 40" (.9m and 1m) is available.

The most commonly sold cloth is known as E-glass, and is what you will get unless there is another designation. There is also a six-ounce cloth known as S-glass or S-cloth. It is purported to be stronger, stiffer, and tougher than standard E-glass. The claims for S-glass range from 20% to 100% increase in strength. I have tried it, but it is difficult to tell if a lack of wear and tear on a canoe is the result of strong cloth or just good canoeing skills and luck. S-glass costs considerably more than E-glass, so the way you plan to use your canoe should help you decide if the extra expense is justified.

The intended use for your canoe will not only determine the kind of fiberglass cloth you may want to use, but also the amount. The two extremes range from season after season of pounding down rocky rivers, such as I did in my guiding business, to occasional use by one or two people on a quiet little pond or stream. Unless I was really trying to shave down the weight, I almost always used one layer outside with a football-shaped piece for the bottom, thus doubling the protection there. One

layer is usually sufficient for the inside. I built one of my 16' (4.9m) Wabnakis to be as light as possible. For this canoe I used only one layer of 6-ounce cloth outside and a layer of 2-ounce cloth inside. To further cut down on the weight, I made the gunwales and decks of cedar instead of hardwood. The only hardwood in the canoe is in the seats and the carrying yoke. This 16' (4.9m) canoe weighs less than 45 pounds (20kg), but is plenty strong enough for its intended purpose.

Most builders don't make their canoe for knocking around in whitewater. So, the amount of material you will need depends on how you plan to use your canoe. For the average user, a 6-ounce layer plus a 6-ounce football piece on the outside and a single layer in the inside should do it. After you decide on the number of layers of cloth you will need, multiply that number by the length of the canoe. Since fiberglass cloth is sold by the yard, you will need to divide that number by three. Order a narrower length if you plan to use a football-shaped piece. You will have scraps of cloth after the fiberglassing is finished. Save some of this for future repairs and other projects.

Kevlar

If you know that you will be giving your canoe some hard use in whitewater, you may want to consider adding some extra protection to save you future repairs. A football-shaped piece of Kevlar will make a big difference in the amount of abuse your canoe will withstand.

Kevlar is available in a variety of forms: stitched triaxial, stitched non-woven, felt, and others. It also comes in a variety of weights. Probably the Kevlar felt is the best choice for armor plating the bottom of a canoe. This felt has been sold for a long time by companies like Old Town Canoe for applying an abrasion-resistant skid plate on the bow and stern of their plastic and composite canoes.

It would be nice to say that using Kevlar is as easy as fiberglassing, but that is not the case. When you order your material, be sure to order the special scissors along with it. This material is almost impossible to cut without the very sharpest of tools. You will usually have the choice of two or more weights of Kevlar. To be safe, I used the heaviest for my canoe and it proved to be overkill. Another canoe I did later with a lighter version worked out just as well, and didn't add as much weight. Because the material is quite expensive, you will want to make maximum use of what you buy.

You do not need a continuous piece of Kevlar to cover the bottom. The following is an example of how I did mine. Say you want to cover the bottom, 36 inches (914mm)-wide at the widest point, and you want to cover a total of 17 feet (5.2 meters) of an 18-foot (5.5 meter) canoe. If you are careful while wetting it out, you can butt pieces of the material together so the seam is almost invisible. So, if the Kevlar is 60 inches (1.5 meters)-wide, you will need enough 36-inch by 60-inch (914mm by 1.5m) pieces to cover the required 17 feet (5.2 meters). Seventeen feet equals 204 inches; divide that by 60, and you will see you need 3.4 pieces that are 60 inches by 36 inches. You can safely order 3 yards (108 inches) of the 60-inch material because where the football narrows, you can salvage enough to make up the .4 pieces. Or, if you want extra Kevlar on hand for other projects, order 4 yards.

Be aware that Kevlar will not be transparent as is fiberglass after wetting out, so you will have a rather ugly-looking yellow bottom on your canoe. If you apply the football-shaped covering below the water line, no one will ever know until you take the canoe out of the water. The material wets out similar to fiberglass, perhaps taking a little longer to soak up the resin. You can tell the progress by the color change as the resin soaks in. If you are applying your Kevlar layer as a part of your initial fiberglassing of the hull, you can take advantage of the chemical bond, as mentioned on page 44. If the Kevlar layer is a retrofit, or is being applied after the initial layer of fiberglass has cured, then it will be necessary to sand the cured fiberglass to allow the new resin in the Kevlar to form a mechanical bond. After wetting out, you will need to roll on filler coat(s) of resin until the weave is filled.

You will not be able to sand out and feather the edge of your Kevlar layer. The stuff just will not sand. This is why it is important to make as neat a cut as possible when forming your football's edge.

I have used my 20-foot (6.1-meter) White Guide model with Kevlar for several seasons of guiding on whitewater rivers. I have never had to do a repair on the canoe since the application. I used Kevlar as a retrofit, so it did add some weight to the canoe. If added during the building process, the Kevlar can replace at least one fiberglass layer, and thus should result in a very small weight increase, if any.

Epoxy

Because fiberglass materials are the most expensive items on the whole project, I have tried to be careful in recommending quantities for you to use. The cloth is easy, because it is just a matter of feet and yards, but the resin is another thing. The inconvenience and frustration of running out in the middle of a project is to be avoided as is the expense of buying too much of the stuff. Two layers of cloth uses more resin than one and three more than two, etc. The recommendations here are to assist you in determining how much you will need, but how you customize your canoe will be the final deciding factor. I should mention, however, that once you start using these materials, you will find almost no end of things you can repair and build, so any extra material can be put to good use.

For the 18.5' (5.6m) White Guide Model we built to illustrate this book, we used two and a half gallons of RAKA resin, along with the requisite amount of hardener. So, three gallons of resin and a gallon and a half of hardener would be a prudent buy. This canoe was built with one layer and a football-shaped piece on the outside, and one layer on the inside. Any leftover resin will not go to waste. My experience, borne out by tests by Gougeon Brothers, indicates the resin and hardener has an almost unlimited shelf life. The only change I have noticed is a slight discoloration of the hardener in my older supplies. However, in use there was no difference from a newer batch.

Most epoxies are sold with several hardeners, each with the chemistry best suited for the intended purpose. Also, the hardeners may have to be mixed at a different ratio from others in the supplier's inventory. Since these are things that are subject to change over the years, I will not delve into the subject other than to advise you to read the supplier's literature before making your decision. I do recommend you purchase the no-blush hardener. It will save some frustration. Blush is a waxy substance that rises to the surface of the cured epoxy. It clogs up sandpaper really efficiently unless it is thoroughly washed off—better to not have it in the first place.

Measuring pumps are recommended for WEST System resins because they are mixed at odd ratios—a five-to-one or a three-to-one ratio. These ratios are difficult to measure. Their pumps provide the correct ratio with one stroke of the resin pump and one stroke of the hardener pump. These are especially handy when only a small amount of mixed resin is needed. RAKA's pumps all dispense the same amount of material from each pump, so for a two-to-one ratio you would use two strokes of the resin pump and one stroke of the hardener pump. When using large quantities of RAKA resin, I simply pour the resin and hardener into a graduated container. For 18 ounces of mixed epoxy, I pour in 12 ounces of resin and then add hardener to bring the total to the 18-ounce mark (6 ounces).

It is possible to mix a five-to-one ratio without the benefit of pumps. Mark a stick with six equally spaced increments equaling the total you will be measuring. Using a container with straight sides (a coffee can for example), pour in the resin up to the fifth mark and then add hardener to the sixth mark.

On the subject of mixing, be sure to do it thoroughly. I always told my students to stir for one full minute. As you stir, scrape the sides of the container occasionally to be sure all of the chemicals are well blended.

The poly mixing pots are reusable and convenient for mixing your resin, but almost any clean metal or plastic container will do as long as you have a way to measure. Be sure to wear disposable gloves whenever handling resin and hardener. You may be sensitive to the chemicals you will be handling or, through repeated exposure, become sensitive. Besides all that, the material is messy and clean up is a lot easier if you simply have to peel off the gloves. The rest of the equipment on the list should be available locally, if you don't have it already. I trust you have read the chapter on safety before proceeding with this chapter; consider the safety precautions as very inexpensive insurance. Also, be sure to read and follow any precautions and instructions that the supplier of the materials may provide.

Silica

In addition to the cloth and epoxy, there are a few other materials that will help make your project easier. I recommend you purchase a small amount of silica. WEST System sells it as colloidal silica and RAKA sells it as fumed silica. This can be used as a general-purpose thickener for the resin and results in a clear, but somewhat milky mixture. It can also be used in conjunction with other material to help thicken. I mentioned the saving of the sanding dust, or cedar flour, in the hull-building chapter. It makes wonderful filler when mixed with epoxy and silica.

Cotton fibers

Most definitely get some cotton fibers, sold as Microfibers by Gougeon. This stuff makes the best waterproof glue you will ever find when mixed with epoxy resin. You put in as much or as little as you need for the consistency you need. It has great gap-filling properties and so will help fill and cover a variety of mistakes (there are bound to be some). It will be white when cured, but here again you can add a little cedar flour for color.

Tools

The list of tools you will need is based on the assumption that there will be two people doing the job. Thus, two roller frames will be enough. They can be wiped off and used over and over. Just be sure to get them as clean as possible between uses so the rollers keep working.

There is an extra roller pan on the list in case one gets too fouled up to use. If you drain them thoroughly after use, the remaining cured epoxy will not interfere with future use. If necessary, they should be available locally.

The 12 roller covers should be sufficient, but it doesn't hurt to buy a few extras. They cannot be re-used.

The squeegees are the least expensive and yet the most useful tools for wetting out fiberglass. They are easily cleaned for re-use.

Filling and Sealing

1. Mix up the sealer coat.

Now we're ready to get going. If you filled the screw holes, etc., as suggested in the hull-building chapter, you are ready for the sealer coat, which is necessary to prevent the cedar from sucking the resin away from your fabric when you start to apply the cloth. This sealer coat will also do some filling. Mix up 18 ounces or more of resin and hardener. Add enough cedar flour to give it a rich brown color, but not enough to thicken too much. You will apply this sealer coat with rollers, so the resin must be a liquid.

2. Roll and squeegee.

It is best to have two people working: one to roll on the mixture, and one to squeegee it off. To start, give the mixture a minute or two to soak in, and then remove all you can with the squeegee. Save the stuff in a container—it can be reused. Squeegee off as much material as possible. The best technique for the squeegee is to remove the bulk of the material in a section of the canoe, saving it in a container for future use. Then go back over that same section, wiping the squeegee dry with a paper towel each time you make a pass. If the material you save starts to get a little thick, do not try to reuse it, but mix up another batch to continue. Continue rolling and squeegeeing until you have the entire hull sealed. Try not to leave any resin on the surface of the hull. You will see the staple holes and other minor openings beautifully filled in with the mixture, and you will see the true color of your canoe for the first time. While your sealer coating is still wet, it is okay to proceed with the stem reinforcement, the instructions for which are provided on page 46. Doing this at this time saves you waiting yet another day for the material to cure.

When resin and hardener are mixed, an exothermic (heat producing) polymerization reaction has begun. At room temperature, the ingredients will appear to stay in the same state as when they were first mixed for the duration of the pot life. This can vary from 15 to 40 minutes, depending on the hardener used and the temperature of the material and of the room. Thereafter, the mixture will thicken, beginning visibly to change from a liquid

to a solid material. In five to nine hours, the epoxy mixture reaches a partial cure, being relatively free of tackiness. It can be sanded and shaped in 15 to 20 hours. At this point it will appear that the reaction is complete, but actually there is a residual reaction, which continues for the next five to seven days, causing the epoxy to become harder.

A number of factors can influence the cure schedule described above, and since I have no way to know conditions under which you will be working, I think it is important that you understand them.

The most important factor is that, in an exothermic reaction such as this, the speed of the reaction can be accelerated by adding heat to it and conversely, can be slowed down by withdrawing heat. For instance, if you are mixing epoxy on a hot day, you will find the reaction to be faster than anticipated; pot life is shorter and cure-up occurs much more rapidly. On the other hand, if you are working in a cold atmosphere, pot life will be slightly longer and cure-up time will be extended. The ambient temperature is helping to accelerate the reaction in the first instance and, in the second, is causing catalytic heat to be dissipated to the atmosphere more rapidly, thus slowing down the reaction.

The heat that is being created chemically in your resin can dissipate more rapidly if it is spread out than it can when left standing in a container. So, the sooner you get the resin spread onto the canoe, the more working time you will have. Remember, too, that your roller pan has many times the surface area that the mixing pot has, and so it will be a better place for the unused resin to stay as you work. The more confined the container, the faster the catalytic heat will build up.

To summarize and simplify this problem of temperature, plan on an 18 to 24 hour cure time between the application and when you want to work on it, such as sanding. I like the room temperature (and the materials as well) to be as near to 75° F (24° C) as possible. At a higher temperature, you will have to be aware of a faster cure time. At a lower temperature you will find the resin thicker and more difficult to spread. The result can be runs and using more material than is necessary.

Roll on the sealer/filler coat. Allow it to soak in a minute or so before the squeegeeing begins. You can be generous with the resin mix here, because the resin that is squeegeed off can be reused until it starts to thicken (cure).

Use the squeegee to remove the excess resin mix. Here, Jason is angling the squeegee like a snowplow so the excess resin will pile up toward the wet side, leaving the dry side relatively clear of it.

Go over the hull with the squeegee again. Here, Kelly is going over a section that was previously done. She is wiping the squeegee after each pass to ensure that none of the resin picked up is deposited back on the canoe.

Stem Reinforcement

3

Add end reinforcement. Once the hull is completely sealed and squeegeed as dry as possible, you can add the end reinforcement. Lay the strip of fiberglass cloth over the point and up over the canoe. Make two or three slits to facilitate making the cloth lie flat.

Because I do not use a wooden stem piece for strip canoes (I think I covered the subject pretty well in the hull-building chapter), it is a good idea to apply some additional reinforcement in the form of an extra layer of fiberglass fabric. As I mentioned before, this can be done while the sealer coat is still wet.

1. Cut strips of fiberglass cloth.

You will need two strips (one for each end) of fiberglass fabric about 4" (102mm) wide and 3' to 3½' (.9m to 1m) long. If the only cloth you have is what you bought in the 60" (1.5m) width, just cut a strip from each side at the end of the fabric. This will make the big piece a little over 50" (1.3m) wide instead of 60" (1.5m). When the cloth is applied to the canoe, there is a lot more fabric than you will need at each end where the canoe narrows, so you are just borrowing what will be cut off later anyway. Fiberglass tape is available in 3", 4", and 6" (76mm, 102mm, and 152mm) widths, which can be used for stem reinforcement if you wish, but there is no necessity for this expense. You have to buy a whole roll. Your scraps will do just as well.

2. Fold the strip over the stem.

The prepared strip should be placed and folded right over the stem, starting at the top (it is the bottom now, though) where it meets the strongback, and should extend well around to the bottom of the canoe, covering the portion of the canoe that will often take a lot of abrasion when the canoe is skidded ashore onto sand and gravel. Another layer could be applied to this area if you wish to have extra protection there.

3. Cut slits in the cloth.

You will have to cut slits in the cloth to make it lie flat around the sharp curve of the stem, but this is normal, and the roughness this creates can be sanded away when you do the general sanding following the sealer coat. The edges of the reinforcement are to be feathered in preparation for the main fiberglassing job, and any other roughness can be smoothed at this time.

4a

Apply resin. The upper part of the reinforcement is completely wetted out, and the lower part is being "tacked" in place with the brush. Whenever working with fabric such as this, always start from the center and work toward the edges.

4b

Use a brush to smooth. The fabric will obediently lie as it should as you work from the center toward the cut edge. In this photo, a little more resin will be applied to the white area above the brush.

4. Apply resin to the strips.

For this relatively small fiberglassing job, a foam or other disposable brush and a squeegee should be the only tools needed. Use the brush to carry the resin to the dry cloth, and the squeegee to smooth out and remove excess resin that will occur. You will learn a little about fiberglassing here as well. Notice how the fabric has a lot of bias "stretch," and by pushing, pulling and teasing it around, you can make it take almost any reasonable shape. Two or three slits in the strips will be sufficient. The "stretch" of the cloth will accommodate the rest of the shaping.

4c

Don't use too much resin. The completed stem reinforcement will look like this. An excessive amount of resin is usually used for things such as this—thus the runs seen at the top of the photo. No problem though; they will be smoothed out later.

Stem Reinforcement (continued)

5

Feather and smooth the cloth. Jason smoothes out the rough edges and feathers the edge of the cloth where it meets the wood. Careful concentration is necessary here to prevent sanding through the sealer coat when feathering.

5. Feather and smooth the cloth.

When the sealer coat and your reinforcing strips have cured (about 24 hours later), smooth out any roughness and feather the edges of the cloth. Be extra careful when feathering not to sand through your sealer coat where the fiberglass strip meets the sealed wood. This feathering and smoothing need not be carried to the extreme of smoothness; the fiberglass to come will act as a screed and cover up a lot of the irregularity. Just be sure there are no rough edges to catch the fabric or create bubbles under the next layer of fabric that you are soon to apply. Now you are ready for the main event.

6. Sand the sealer coat.

Sand the sealer coat well to ensure a good bond by your fiberglass, which is the step coming right up. Use 80-grit sandpaper for this and be sure you completely cover the surface. You should have ruined that pretty look and now have a dull, milky surface that is well-scratched with the 80 paper so that it has the teeth to hold the next step, but don't sand so much that you get down to untreated wood. The surface of the hull will not look very good, but will feel smooth to the hand without any fuzzy feeling or hardened dust particles. If you are not satisfied with your sealer coat, it can be repeated at this time and will use a minimal amount of material. However, this second sealing is seldom needed, and you should not find it necessary. Epoxy resin has an amazing ability to penetrate the tiniest opening (including wood pores), and when you are finished with the outside of your canoe and start smoothing up the inside, you will see where small amounts of resin have penetrated all the way through some small openings you didn't think existed.

Fiberglassing the Hull

1. Prepare the extra bottom layer if desired.
If you plan to use the football-shaped piece on the bottom, lay the cloth in place and cut it to shape.

2. Drape and trim the fiberglass.
Next just drape the fiberglass fabric over the canoe, cutting the end so that there are about 6" of fabric extending beyond both stems when the cloth is held up so the weave runs fairly straight (not draping down over the ends, which could cause you to cut it too short). You will see already that the fabric tends to assume the shape of the hull. There will be some waves in the cloth near the gunwale area; take care of this by tugging gently at the fabric from up near the stems. In fact, do everything dealing with this cloth gently and you will avoid wrinkles, crinkles and waves that result when a hard yank pulls the weave out of line. Once this happens, it is hard to correct, and the cloth will defy you every step of the way. The full layer of cloth will hang below the gunwales. Trim it off at this time to just a couple of inches below the gunwales. As you approach the ends with your trimming, have someone hold up the center of the cloth level with the bottom of the canoe so that you do not trim off too much. If you are doing more than one layer, simply put the next layer right over the first and trim as described above. Multiple fiberglass layers are wet out all at once. The more layers you have, the longer it will take to wet out, but it will wet out.

Prepare the extra bottom layer. The sealer coating has been sanded and we are ready to start the main event. Here the football-shaped piece is ready on the hull.

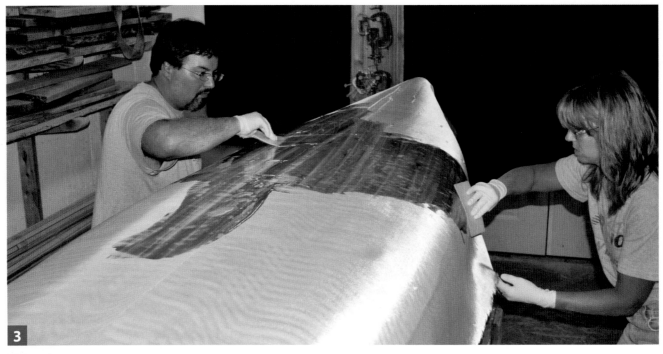

3

Wet out the fiberglass. The fabric is all in place, trimmed to a couple of inches below the gunwales. Jason and Kelly have started the wetting out. The resin was poured in the middle of the canoe and they work it down and out (toward the ends) with their squeegees.

3. Wet out the fiberglass.

Now you and your partner can put on your gloves and start wetting out the fabric. You will definitely need squeegees, and when you get to the ends you will need disposable brushes. Plastic should be spread below the canoe to protect the floor—there will be drips! Pour the mixed epoxy right in the middle of the canoe and start spreading it with the squeegees. The cloth is wet out when it becomes transparent and you see the beautiful wood below. With the squeegees, drag the resin puddle to the dry areas of cloth, working down toward the gunwales and toward one end. With a little practice you will be able to take the resin all the way to the gunwale and lose hardly a drop. Press down hard enough with the squeegees—actually drag it to a dry area—so as to remove any excess resin that will try to build up under the cloth. The resin will float the cloth if you allow too much to accumulate. At the same time, be aware that it is possible to bear down too hard with the squeegee. If you see a faint whiteness on the surface of the cloth behind your squeegee, you are actually wringing too much resin out of the cloth. Just go back over it with a little more resin. The squeegees are held at about

a 45 degree or less angle to the surface. As you drag resin toward the gunwales, you can flatten the squeegee to press the resin into the cloth and prevent the excess from dripping off the edge. You will be surprised how quickly you get the hang of this squeegeeing!

Subsequent batches of resin can be applied where needed. The best way is to work from the bottom middle of the canoe down toward the gunwales, and then out toward one of the ends: down and out. If you make the mistake of doing the bottom (the easy part) all the way to the ends before wetting out down to the gunwales, you will have trouble with bubbles, wrinkles, and waves. Another good rule to remember is to never leave a dry area between areas that have been wet out. If you do run into trouble with a bubble or wrinkle, take care of it right away; don't leave it to do later. You should never have to, but if all else fails, cut a slit in the fabric to make it lie down. The edges can be feathered later so it will be invisible. Waves along the gunwales can be smoothed, as I explained before, by walking to the ends and gently tugging the wave out of the cloth. Sometimes you can smooth them with your hand, moving from the center toward the ends.

4. Bring the fiberglass around the ends of the canoe.

When you are within about a foot of the end of the canoe, you have to do something about bringing the fabric around the ends. Pause in your wetting out to prepare the end of the cloth. The first thing that is obvious is that a slit must be cut along the centerline of the cloth until it reaches the point where the cloth is in smooth contact with the center of the canoe. However, don't cut it exactly on the center. Make the cut about 1 or 1½ inches (25 or 38mm) to one side. You'll see the wisdom in this when you wet it out and start to bring the cloth around the sharp end of the canoe. If the cut is made exactly in the center, the cloth will not behave and lie down where it is supposed to be.

5. Wet out one side of the cloth at the ends.

Next, wet out one side completely to the end, but do not try to bring it around yet. If you are applying two complete layers, work with one layer at a time in this area. Just fold the top layer back out of the way for the time being. Now cut off the side you just wetted out so that it follows the stem line of the canoe and reaches about 2 inches (51mm) beyond it. A disposable brush is a good tool here to carry the resin to the cloth and to assist in bringing the 2-inch (51mm) extension of cloth around the stem to the other side. Bring this extra cloth around and tack it in place with resin at about 6 inch (152mm) intervals along the stem line. This done, you should have a series of bulges between the places where you have tacked the cloth in place. Using your brush, make the cloth go into place around the stem without making a single slit in the cloth. Using plenty of resin here helps; you can squeegee off the excess later. Remember, you can push and pull the cloth a little with your brush to make it stretch into place. If you do have a lot of trouble with this technique, go ahead and make a slit or two. It will still come out all right.

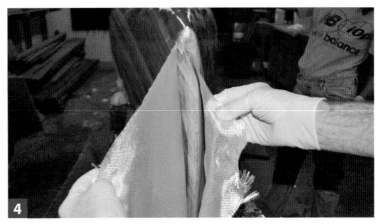

Bring the fiberglass around the ends of the canoe. The ends require some special attention. Split the cloth slightly off center. If you are doing two complete layers, then handle them one at a time at this point.

Wet the cloth out to the end. Use a brush to carry the resin to the cloth, then cut off the fabric about two inches beyond the end of the canoe. Notice that the other side is folded back out of the way for the time being.

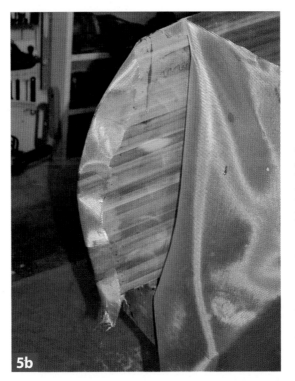

Tack down the cloth. Bring the trimmed fabric around the end and tack it down as we did with the reinforcement previously. However, here we do not have to cut slits to tease the cloth into place. Gently pushing and pulling with the brush will cause the cloth to lie down, as it should. If you do have to cut a slit, no problem.

Fiberglassing the Hull (continued)

Handle the other side the same as the first. A little extra care is required at this stage to avoid disturbing the layer already wetted out as we tease this layer into place. Here I have most of it down while Jason finishes up the other side with the squeegee.

Apply a small patch where the slit made in the photo 5a ends. This ensures good coverage here. The cloth could be extended 12" to 18" (305mm to 457mm) toward the center of the canoe if you want a little more protection for this area that is sometimes scraped on a rocky shoreline.

Filling the cloth

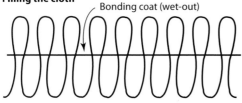

Bonding coat (wet-out)

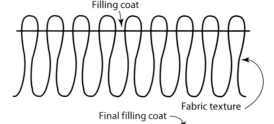

Filling coat

Fabric texture

Final filling coat

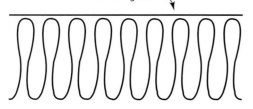

Figure 5-1: Wetting out. This drawing shows graphically the wetting out and filling of the fiberglass fabric. In some cases only one filler coat will do the job. Remember, more resin equals more weight!

6. Complete the second side of the cloth ends.

Cut the other side of the cloth the same way and bring it around the stem as you did the first side, being careful not to disturb the fabric you already have in place from the first side. If you are doing two complete layers, then just repeat the process for the second layer. It is a good idea to make the centerline cut of this second layer on the opposite side from the first layer. Things will lie better and make a stronger job. When the end is complete there will be a rough edge where the last end comes around, but this can be taken care of later by feathering out the edge with a sander.

7. Apply patches to the ends.

There is always some roughness, and sometimes gaps, in the fiberglass where the slits you cut in the cloth ends. It is a good idea to cut a small 2½" x 4" (64mm x 102mm) patch from your scrap pieces of fiberglass and apply it over this area.

8. Fix bubbles and waves.

When both ends are complete, you should look the hull over closely for areas where there might be too little resin (whitish on the surface) or too much resin (little waves or shiny areas). Look for bubbles and waves along the gunwales where the cloth might have lifted from the hull while you were busy elsewhere. Everything you can fix now will save a lot of work after the resin has cured. It does no harm to work with the material right up to the point at which it hardens so much that you can't work with it. If, in spite of your diligence, you have bubbles, don't be overly concerned. They can be sanded out, patched and then feathered down so they will never show.

9. Check for matte finish.

When the wetting out process is finished, the surface should have a matte finish; there should be few, or no, shiny spots indicating an excess of resin. If you see any such spots, use the squeegee to take care of the problem. The fabric is now completely saturated with resin, but the weave is only one-half to two-thirds filled. The filling is completed in subsequent coatings of resin. See **Figure 5-1**.

10. Pick chemical or mechanical bond.

Epoxy bonds to itself in two ways. To put a layer of material over one that has cured (24 hours or more) requires that the cured surface be sanded (scratched up in good shape) so the new material can make a good mechanical bond. In order to get a good chemical bond, the new layer must be applied before the previous layer has completely cured. The chemical bond is preferred and so you must stand by and keep testing the filled fiberglass until it is ready. It is ready when it does not feel sticky to the touch, but you can dent it with your fingernail. If you must leave it longer, then wait 24 hours and sand completely with 80 grit before applying a filler coating.

11. Apply filler coat.

When you are ready for the filler coating, mix up a batch of resin and roll it completely over the hull. Now the surface starts to be shiny. The one roller coating may be enough. If not, wait 24 hours and sand, or wait until it is to the stage for chemical bonding and apply another coat with the rollers.

12. Sand the hull.

When you have the weave completely filled, the hull will be a smooth, shiny, beautiful thing to behold. You'd like to leave it that way, but it is not to be. It has to be sanded to prepare the surface for a protective coat of ultraviolet filtered varnish (polyurethane). If you sanded between filler coats, you should have taken care of the rough edges where you brought the cloth around the stems. If you went for the chemical bond, then you can do it when you do the general sanding. You will want to use 80 grit followed with 100 or 120 grit. If you have done a good job of filling, you should be able to sand the hull to a nice smooth surface without sanding into the fabric (except where you will feather out the cloth at the stems). You can use the same sanding material that body shops use for wet sanding in auto body repair. It gives a good smooth finish and a good surface to hold the polyurethane, and it produces no dust. Wait until the canoe is finished to apply the polyurethane, because you will be handling it a lot before it is ready to go out the door. Better to get the first scratches on the river.

10

Pick a chemical or mechanical bond. If you are able to wait for the resin to reach the stage for a chemical bonding of the filler coat (not sticky to touch, but can be dented with the fingernail) you can avoid this sanding. In this case we had to wait 24 hours before starting the sealer coatings so we had to sand.

11

Roll on the filler coat. Now look how nice and shiny the canoe has become. If a second filler coat is needed, you either must do the same sanding for a mechanical bond or stand by to get the chemical bond. In any case, sand the last filler coat, because the hull will eventually be coated with an ultra violet filter polyurethane.

Preparing the Inside

Remove the stations. With the final filler coat on and the hull sanded to a dull, milky finish, the canoe is ready to turn over and stand on its own. You can remove the stations easily. The strongback can be put away—its job is done.

Remove the stem pieces. The stem pieces resist removal. Place a piece of scrap wood down to protect the bottom of the canoe and pry up on the stem piece as Jason is doing here. A hammer or bar may be used.

Finishing up and fiberglassing the inside of your hull is not very much different than doing the outside, but there are a few special problems to overcome. On the premise that you have already been through the preparation of the outside of the hull and are ready to tackle the inside, I have focused this section on the special problems that you may encounter at this stage.

1. Remove the canoe from the stations.
With 24 hours or more passed since you applied the last coat of resin to the outside, and sanded, it is time to go to work again. Now you can take the hull off the stations, for it can support itself.

2. Take out the screws.
Start by taking out the drywall screws where you attached the stations to the strongback. Don't forget the screw you angled up through the stem supports into the stems. The screws through the first and last stations into the stems can remain in place until you turn the canoe over.

3. Lift off the hull.
With all of the screws removed, the hull, along with the stations, can be lifted from the strongback, turned over and placed on top of the strongback right side up. If the stations haven't fallen over already (as they did in the photo above, right), give them a tap or a push and they will come free.

4. Remove the stations and stem pieces.
Now you can remove the screws that hold the first and last stations and the stem pieces together. Remove the stations. The stem pieces do not come out quite as easily. Place a block of wood on the bottom of the canoe right next to the stem piece and then pry up with a crow bar or the hook of a hammer as shown in the photo at left. It will come free, probably leaving some of its tape behind on the hull. The strongback can be stored away now; its job is done for this canoe. The canoe can be supported on the two sawhorses.

Cut the excess fiberglass away from the gunwales. This way, it won't scrape your arms and interfere as you work on the inside. The drawshave works well for this, but any knife will do if you use caution.

5. Cut off the excess fiberglass at the gunwales.

6. Scrape and sand the inside.

Look at that inside—what a mess! You have ahead of you nearly the same job that you had on the outside of the hull. The only difference is that it is a little harder to get at the inside. You will use the same tools: a scraper (the one ground to a curve as shown on page 37), and sanders with 60-grit discs. A rounded profile Surform plane could also be used to help smooth the rounded part of the inside of the hull.

The canoe will slide around now as you work on it, because it no longer has the heavy stations and strongback to anchor it in place. You can overcome this insecurity by having someone hold it for you, or by lodging one end against a wall as you work with the scraper and/or the Surform.

7. Remove excess glue.

The stems are difficult to get to, so do the best you can. A wood chisel can be used to chip away the glue and other debris that hangs on, and hand sanding will finish the job. Sanding smooth right into the point isn't necessary as this area will hardly be visible. As with the outside, try to remove all of the glue inside the hull before turning to the sanders.

8. Sand and apply sealer coat.

When you have done as much as possible with the scrapers and Surform, use the sanders with the 60-grit discs and sand the inside smooth. Go ahead with the sealer coat and the same procedure as with the outside of the hull.

Scrape the inside. As with the outside of the hull, scraping is the best way to remove the excess glue. The rounded scraper gets into the rounded, concave, areas. A Surform plane with a rounded blade also works well here.

Sand the inside. Sanding is dusty business, so we took the opportunity of a pleasant afternoon to sand the inside outdoors. Kelly and Jason are sanding with 60-grit discs on the random orbit sanders.

Keel

In my opinion, a keel is an abomination on a canoe, but if you insist on having one now is the time to do it. I have no photos to illustrate the process because I do not install them. A keel does keep the canoe running straight, but that is a problem, at least it is for me. Better to learn to keep the canoe running straight with the paddle and enjoy the quick response and ease of turning that a keelless canoe will provide.

1. Prepare the keel.

That said, you will need a strip of hardwood, ash, oak, or other strong wood ¾" (19mm) x ¾" (19mm) x 4 feet (1.2 meters) shorter than your canoe (12' for a 16' canoe). Taper and round off the ends so they more or less follow the line of the stems.

2. Find the centerline of the canoe.

Now turn the hull upside down and snap a chalkline to get the exact center (keel line) of the canoe. Mark where the ends of the keel will reach.

3. Drill holes.

Now drill a series of holes (shank size ³⁄₁₆" [5mm]), along the centerline. Make the first hole about 3" (76mm) from where the end of the keel will be and drill holes every 6" (152mm). On the other end, split the difference on spacing to place your last hole 3" (76mm) from the end.

4. Countersink the holes.

Turn the canoe over and countersink these holes on the inside of the canoe. With the canoe upside down again, measure ⅜" (10mm) (half the thickness of the keel) to one side of your centerline of holes and make a series of clearly visible marks. These marks will provide a visual reference against which to line up the keel as you screw it to the hull.

5. Screw on the keel.

To attach the keel, you'll need one person working from under the hull and one on top. Holding the keel in place along the reference marks, drill a pilot hole with a ³⁄₃₂" (2.5mm) drill bit, and drive home a screw (¾" [19mm] number 8 flathead). Drill and drive the screws as you go along making sure the alignment is correct for each screw. If you work carefully and methodically, your keel will be straight.

6. Remove the keel and sand.

Now, take out all of the screws and remove the keel. If you haven't sanded the outside already, sand to rough up the area where the keel is to lie.

7. Apply resin and keel.

Mix up some resin and apply it on the keel line and on the keel itself. It would be a good idea to mix a little silica with the resin to be sure there are no voids between the hull and the keel. Replace the keel and secure it with the screws. Clean up the excess resin and you now have a permanent and waterproof keel.

Fiberglassing the Inside

Now it's time to fiberglass the interior. As before, the experience you gained in fiberglassing the outside of your hull will stand you in good stead on the inside. The process is exactly the same, so I will only point out the aggravating little problems that may crop up and give some hints as to how to overcome them.

1. Apply a bead of filler to the stems.

Note: This applies only if you do not use a hardwood stem. Before you apply the sealer coat to the inside of the hull, you can do something to improve the looks and strength of the stems. Mix up some resin and add silica and cedar flour until you have a peanut butter consistency. Using a thin rounded stick, apply this mixture right up into the point of the canoe. Make a wide bead of it from about an inch (25mm) below the top all the way to where the canoe starts to widen out—don't go all the way to the top, as it will interfere when you are ready to install the decks. This wide bead of filler will do wonders for the looks of the area and the epoxy mixture will increase the strength of the stems. When the mixture has cured (24 hours), sand it with a coarse sandpaper.

1

Add a bead of filler to the stems. This helps the looks of the canoe and adds a little strength too. Mix up some epoxy with some silica and cedar flour to make a paste of a peanut butter consistency. Lay it in place with a thin, rounded stick. When cured, sand with coarse sandpaper by hand.

Fiberglassing the Inside (continued)

2. Apply the sealer coat to the inside.

Get out your roller and apply the sealer coat as shown on page 45. When you apply the sealer coat of resin, as well as when you are wetting out the cloth and subsequent filler coats, any excess resin will run to the bottom of the canoe, where it will collect in ever thickening layers that, if allowed to harden, will give extra weight to lug around yet add no strength to the canoe. Also, the excess resin will float the cloth much more readily here than on the outside. This situation will show up as waves in the wetted cloth's surface. It does no harm, but adds weight. So, watch for excess resin and keep it cleaned up as best you can. The squeegees are your best tools for moving resin out or to someplace where it is needed. If you want to add a permanent label of some sort, now is the time.

3. Drape and trim the fiberglass.

Next, drape the fiberglass inside the canoe, as discussed on page 49, and prepare to wet it out. When you are wetting out the fabric, watch for bridging along the bilge area of the hull where the curve is the sharpest. I find I am constantly adjusting the cloth with one hand along the gunwale while I am wetting out with the other. If you get a bridge, squeegee downward from the gunwale, pulling the fabric down and sealing the cloth to the hull in the offending spot.

Spread the cloth over the interior. Smooth it out with your hands. Leave the ends as-is until the wetting out is done to within a couple of feet of the points. Leave enough cloth to reach into the stems. No trimming along the gunwales until after the wetting out is complete.

Apply the sealer coat. With the inside completely sanded, roll on the epoxy and cedar flour mixture on the inside. The bead in the point of the stem can be seen in this photograph.

2a

Squeegee the inside. Kelly is squeegeeing off the excess on the inside. She will go over it again, wiping the squeegee after each pass with a paper towel to ensure no resin is left on the surface.

2b

Add permanent identification to your canoe. Spread a little resin on the hull and stick the paper to it. The fiberglass will cover it and make it permanent. These can be made on a computer with a laser printer.

This canoe was built, and is owned, by
Jason and Kelly Garland
2009
Photos of its construction were used to illustrate the second edition of
Building A Strip Canoe
by Gil Gilpatrick.

2c

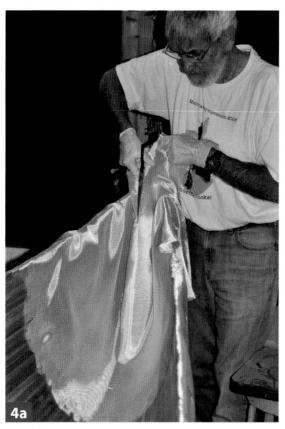

4a

Split the inside ends. Like the outside, the inside ends must be split down the middle. Make this cut back to about where the canoe starts to flatten out. The inside ends are a little time consuming so don't have too much resin mixed up on hand. It may start to cure before you are ready for it.

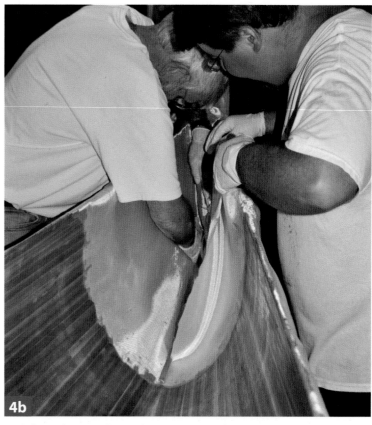

4b

Mark the end to cut to fit into the stem. The cloth from one side is forced into the stem where it is to ultimately go. Run a pencil down the point, marking the cloth. No attempt is made to bring the cloth around as we did on the outside—not necessary.

4. Fiberglass the stems.

When you get to the stems, don't try to bring the cloth around as you did on the outside. Just bring it to the point and trim it there. This is done by first splitting the cloth as you did on the outside. Next, push the cloth into the point, one side at a time, and then run a pencil down the point making a mark on the cloth. Simply cut along this curved line and lay the cloth back in place. If you don't cover all of the wood with the cloth at the very point, don't worry about it. The resin will seal the wood and the extra strength of the fiberglass is not needed in this area. An excessive amount of resin will be used to wet out the cloth in this area carried to the cloth with a disposable brush. Be prepared to clean up the run-off that will collect in the bottom if you don't want a half-inch (13mm) or so of extra thickness there. If you have no use for the excess resin that collects at the bottom, use paper towels to soak it up and remove it. When you're ready, apply the filler coats.

4c

Make the curved cut. With the pencil mark in place, pull the cloth back out and make the curved cut. Repeat for the other side. If some of the wood is not covered with fiberglass fabric in the stems, it is not serious, as long as you protect the wood with resin.

Fiberglassing the Inside (continued)

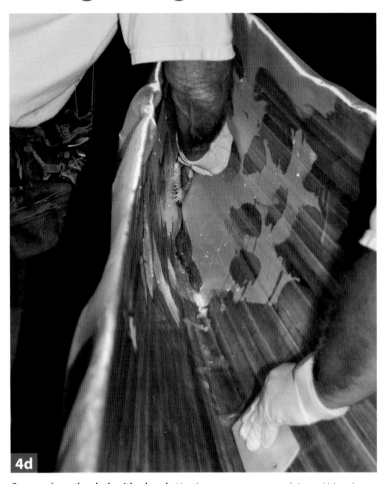

4d

Carry resin to the cloth with a brush. Use the squeegee to smooth it out. Using the brush with a daubing motion ensures the fabric stays where you want it. Pulling with the brush or squeegee could move it.

My final bit of advice for fiberglassing the inside is to have patience. I wish I could say it is a snap, but in fact it can be frustrating. The cloth that smoothed out so nicely over the convex hull on the outside will wrinkle up and fold on the inside if you try to hurry the process. Start out in the middle of the canoe as you did on the outside, and take care of each problem as it occurs, smoothing out the cloth and gently tugging it into place as you apply the resin. It is a good idea to mix the resin in smaller batches after the first batch or two because of the extra time involved.

4f

4e

Remove excess resin. Excess resin will collect near the ends. If it isn't needed, you can remove and discard it by sopping it up with paper towels.

The inside is completely wetted out. Trim the excess cloth at the gunwales (as close as you want it until the resin has cured). As with the outside, you can apply the filler coat with the chemical bond or wait 24 hours, sand, and do the mechanical bond.

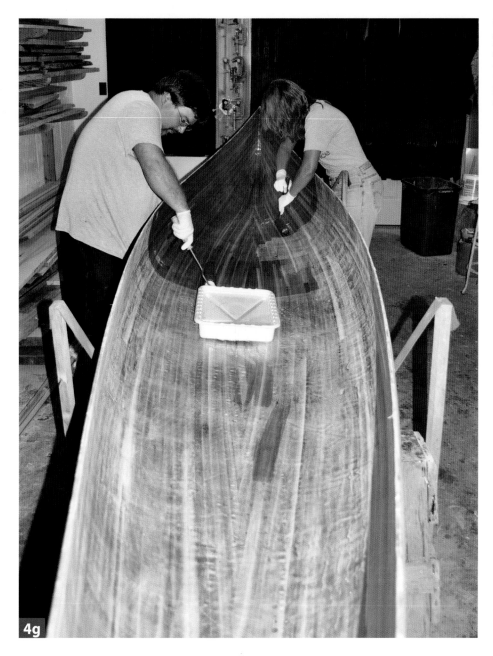

4g

Roll on the filler coat. Jason and Kelly roll on a filler coat after the inside has been sanded. While the chemical bond is theoretically better, I have never had a failure of the mechanical bond; so don't become overly concerned about this matter.

In Conclusion

I hope this chapter has given you the confidence to go ahead with the process of fiberglassing, which is the most challenging, intimidating, and unforgiving of the whole canoe building process. It is worth the time and small expense to cut off a small square of cloth and mix up a little resin to experiment on a piece of scrap wood. Then you can go on to the stem reinforcements which are on a little larger scale, but still not too awesome. After that, move on with confidence to the larger challenge.

I hope I haven't scared you away with all my dire warnings, but I just wanted you to be prepared. Remember, I had 16 and 17 year-old high school students doing this for nearly 30 years. You can do it!

Adding well-built woodwork strengthens your canoe so it can withstand use and abuse.

Chapter 6

The Woodwork

I have watched a lot of capsized canoes suffer the indignity of being swamped and finding their own way—bumping, grinding, and scraping over rocks and ledges—as they get through the rapids (if their owners were lucky) to quieter water, where they slowed up and waited to be recovered. The canoes that have the best chance of surviving this ordeal relatively unscathed were not necessarily those with super-rugged hulls, but rather, those with a strong, well-put-together framework—the woodwork, consisting of the gunwales and thwarts. Without the rigidity of this framework, any canoe is subject to twisting, racking, and bending. Most hulls do not withstand this kind of treatment very well.

The woodwork for your canoe consists of four parts. The gunwales, pronounced "gunnels," sometimes called rails, run along the top edges of the canoe. The decks are pieces of wood that fit into the front and rear corners of the canoe. The thwarts and/or yoke are reinforcing crossbeams near the top of the canoe, with the yoke being shaped to fit a person's shoulders so they can portage the canoe easily. The final parts are the seats. The seats will

be discussed only briefly in this chapter; they are a separate project described later. The caned seats are a rather time consuming project, so if you can read ahead and talk someone into doing them as the canoe is under construction, they will be ready to go when the canoe is done.

Wood

Canoe makers use a wide variety of woods for the woodwork. It depends on what part of the country they live in, their own personal preference, and the intended purpose of the canoe. Probably the most common wood found in Maine for this purpose is white ash. The ash is strong, bends well, and is relatively lightweight. Oak is sometimes used. It is as strong, or stronger, than ash; it is a little heavier, though. Other hardwoods—maple, birch, cherry and mahogany—have been used, and they serve the purpose well. Mahogany is an exotic, and I'm not sure if it fits the hardwood category as we know it, but it is often used.

Gunwales

Spruce is a popular wood for gunwales because of its high strength-to-weight ratio. However, spruce, like mahogany, is rather soft, and does not stand up well to the abrasion of sliding on and off a roof rack of a car. You will quickly discover that the problem isn't what kind of hardwood to use for your gunwales, but where to find stock that is long enough, especially if you are building an 18- or 20-foot (5.5- or 6.1-meter) canoe. The most reliable source for long hardwood boards are sawmills located where there is boat building going on. In these areas, the sawmills cater to the boat builders by sawing long logs to provide the lengths they need. You will seldom find the long lumber you need in a local lumberyard that serves builders and homeowners, although this might be a good place to start your search as they are in tune with the industry.

Yoke and thwarts

For the yoke and thwarts, use most any strong hardwood. For the canoe used to illustrate this book, we used cherry. These parts, like the seats, are subjected to all kind of stress, and you need their strength as cross braces. I often find myself stepping on them when I am climbing over the gear of my loaded canoe when going ashore. If they are not strong enough for this treatment, they are not strong enough.

Decks

For the decks, a variety of woods can be used. I have heard of some builders using fancy figured walnut for this purpose. I usually recommend matching the rest of the woodwork, but this isn't important, except to the canoe owner. A softwood can be used for the decks if that suits your purpose. As I mentioned earlier, I have used cedar for gunwales and decks to cut down on weight, but this is unusual and hardwood gunwales are best in most cases.

Hardware

For hardware you can use brass, bronze, or plain old steel. I have used all three, and for my purposes anyway, the plain old steel available from the local hardware store does just fine. The brass or bronze might be justified in a saltwater environment, but for other uses, I have never had any problem with common hardware. I have listed a supply source in the Appendix for brass and bronze boat-building hardware if you want to go that route.

Materials and tools needed to complete the woodwork
(Quantities will vary with canoe length)

Materials

- Hardwood to make four ¾" x ¾" (19mm x 19mm) gunwales 6" to 12" (152mm to 305mm) longer than the canoe
- Hardwood board ¾" or ⅞" thick (19mm or 22mm), 7" (178mm) wide, 30" (762mm) long for decks
- Hardwood board ¾" or ⅞" thick (19mm or 22mm), 5" (127mm) wide, 36" (914mm) long for yoke
- 2 hardwood boards ¾" or ⅞" thick (19mm or 22mm), 2" (51mm) wide for thwarts
- 100 flathead wood screws, #8, 1½" (38mm) long
- 4 flathead wood screws, #10, 2" (51mm) long
- 8 flathead wood screws, # 10, 1½" (38mm) long
- 4 to 8 (depending on canoe length) flathead machine screws, 10-24, 2" (51mm) long, with nuts and washers
- Carriage bolts to hang seats, ¼" (6mm): Two 6" (152mm) long, six 4" (102mm) long, with nuts and washers
- Paste wax (or soap) to lube screw threads
- Epoxy for glue
- Cotton fibers for glue
- 80-grit sanding discs
- 120-grit sanding discs
- 2 quarts of UV filtered, exterior, glossy polyurethane

Tools

- Table saw
- Electric hand drill/driver
- Band saw
- Saber saw
- Random orbit sander
- Rule
- Handsaw
- Surform plane with flat blade
- 6, hopefully more, C-clamps
- Screwdriver
- Countersink
- ⁵⁄₁₆" (8mm) drill bit
- ³⁄₁₆" (5mm) drill bit
- Combination drill bit to make countersunk holes for 1½" (38mm) #8 flathead wood screws
- 1 or 2 varnish brushes

The Gunwales

The gunwales serve as the foundation for the rest of the woodwork, and so they are the first to be installed. They don't require much material in terms of board feet, but they do have to be long. If a search for long lumber proves fruitless, consider the following: You can splice up your gunwales from shorter stock. The photos at bottom show how to make a splice that is strong and has worked well for me on a number of canoes. The long splice glued together, using epoxy glue you make up yourself with epoxy and cotton fibers, is strong and will serve long and well. For best results, mount the glued-up gunwales with the long splice visible from the side, not the top. Also, try to keep the splice(s) toward the center of the canoe so they are not subjected to the sharp bend at the bow and stern. Also, break the splices. That is, do not allow the splice on the outside gunwale to line up with the splice on the inside gunwale. If you follow these common sense guidelines, I think you will be more than satisfied with your glued-up gunwales.

All four gunwales should be ¾" x ¾" (19mm x 19mm). A wider gunwale can be used on the outside if desired, but the one described above will serve well. Plan on a gunwale length of at least a foot longer than the canoe you are building. You can measure carefully along the sheer line of your canoe if you need to get a more exact measurement.

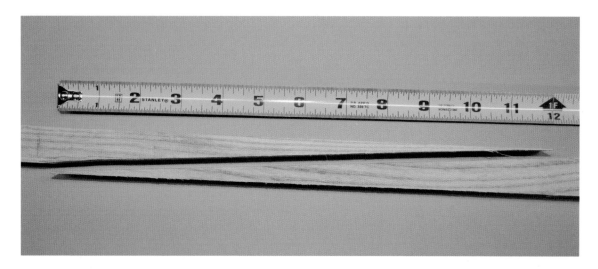

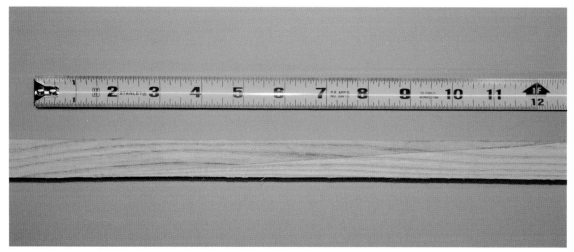

How to make a long splice. This will do the job if you cannot find long lumber for the gunwales. Use a fairly runny glue made of epoxy resin and cotton fibers. Use only moderate pressure with the clamps so as not to squeeze out all the glue. Mount the gunwales so the splice is visible from the side, not the top.

Epoxy the gunwales. Kelly and Jason cover three sides of the gunwales with epoxy resin. This prevents the wood from turning black (and eventually rotting) when water seeps between the gunwale and the fiberglass hull. The uncoated side will be up, or out, when the gunwale has been mounted on the canoe.

1. Epoxy the gunwales.

When your gunwales are ready, coat three sides with epoxy resin to prevent rotting. The uncoated side will be the top side, which will be sanded and polyurethaned eventually. Use the resin in a tray instead of a pot. This is to slow down the exothermic (heat producing) reaction by providing more surface area, allowing the heat to escape more readily—thus, more working time.

2. Mark the gunwale screw positions.

To install the gunwale strips on the hull, start by holding the inwale (inside) strip where it is to go and trim it to a rough (slightly too long) length. A couple of inches short of the point of the stems will be fine for now. While you are holding the inwale in place, mark the center. The center of the canoe is located at the row of staple holes where the center station was located. Cut the other inwale strip the same length. Lay both strips on the floor and, measuring outward from the center, make a mark every 6 inches (152mm). These marks indicate the positions

---

Drill Countersink

I recommend you purchase a combination drill-countersink (some are sold under the trade name of Screw-Mate). If you do, you can proceed as described. If you are drilling shank holes, pilot holes, and countersinking in separate operations, you should drill the shank holes and countersink the inwales before clamping them in place on the canoe. This way you will only have to drill the pilot holes after the gunwales have been clamped in place.

The Gunwales (continued)

4a

Screw the gunwale strips to the hull. When the screws are in place on this end, remove the clamps and clamp up the other end. The drill bit in the drill lying on the canoe bottom is a combination bit that drills the pilot hole, shank hole, and countersink all in one operation for a given screw (in this case 1½" [38mm]).

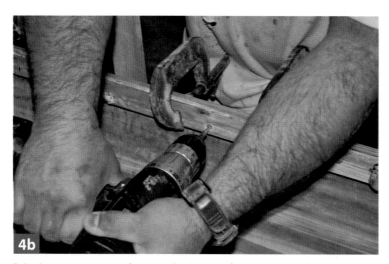

4b

Drive in screws to secure the gunwales. Use care if you use a power driver. The screws are easily snapped off. On this job we found three broken and never realized it until we checked with a hand screwdriver.

of the screws that will hold the gunwales in place.

3. Clamp the gunwale strips to the hull.
Starting at the center of the canoe, use C-clamps to hold the inside and outside gunwale strips along the sheer line. I like to leave ⅛" to ⅛" (2mm to 3mm) of the edge of the hull above the level of the hardwood strips to ensure a nice, level surface when the top surface of the gunwale is smoothed up. Position the clamps between the marks where you have to drill (or the holes you have drilled) so that you'll have room to use the drill and driver. You probably should have six or eight C-clamps for this operation; more would be better. At any rate, clamp as far as your clamps allow, then drill and drive the screws; move the clamps along, repeating the process to the end. Where the sheer line is fairly flat, one clamp between every other mark should be sufficient; where the line curves, you will need a clamp between every mark. Keep the strips even with each other and slightly below the top of the sheer line.

4. Drill pilot holes and attach the gunwale.
For hardware you will need 1½" (38mm) number 8 flathead screws. Philips head is recommended. Buy a box of 100 for the job. When the holes have been drilled, drive the screws in place. You should use some lubrication on the threads. A paste wax works best, but lacking that, scrape some bar soap on the threads. Even with pilot holes, screws drive hard in hardwood. When using a power driver it is very easy to snap screws off, even with lubrication. Check them with a hand screwdriver to ensure they are whole before removing the clamps. If you are using brass or bronze screws, it is even easier to break them off.

5. Sand the gunwale tops.
When the gunwale strips are in place, you may want to dress down the top of the gunwales, bringing the top edge of the fiberglassed hull to the level of the hardwood gunwale strips, stopping short of the deck areas. This will lessen the chance of cutting yourself on the sharp fiberglass edges as well as make the canoe a little easier to handle. A belt sander works best for this job, but a Surform and random orbit sander will do the job as well.

The Decks

1. Cut and apply temporary crosspieces.

You have probably already noticed that your canoe is narrower at the top than it is supposed to be. The inside fiberglassing combined with the gunwales have caused the top to narrow. Before you start to make your decks, cut one or two crosspieces the correct length (the width of your canoe) to temporarily spread the canoe to the correct width. This width at the inside center is that of the middle station. You can see those speaders in the photo at right.

2. Make a cardboard deck template.

Instead of tracing directly from the canoe to the wood of your deck material, I recommend you make a pattern of cardboard or thin plywood. Trace the inside of the canoe where the deck will be installed and cut it out. Next, try it to see if you are satisfied the angle is correct. Adjust as necessary. The inside of the canoe at the point may be a little rough. If so, smooth it up with a fine rasp before making your tracing. Once you determine the angle, the sides of the pattern can be straightened out with a straightedge, even though the sides of the canoe are not ruler-straight. Later, when you screw the decks in place, the flexible canoe will pull in to close any gaps.

3. Cut out the decks.

When you are satisfied with the pattern, cut out the decks. They do not yet have the notches for the inwales that appear in the photos; these you will make next. The total length of most decks is 12 or 14 inches (305mm or 356mm). A ¾"-thick (19mm) deck material will work, but if you can manage to find the desired wood in ⅞" or 1" (22mm or 25mm) thickness, it will be even better.

Cut and apply temporary crosspieces. This photo shows the spreaders in place while we install the decks. Spread the canoe to the original width as dictated by the width of the center station. Kelly is filling some minor defects in the wood along with the screw holes we had to do over because of broken screws.

The Decks (continued)

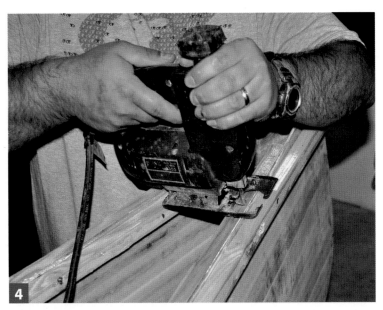

Cut the inwales. Once you decide how far you want the inwale to extend into the deck, trim the ends as Jason is doing. Get them as square as possible and avoid cutting into the hull. Get all of them to the same length by measuring from the point of the stem.

Fit the decks. The outside gunwales have not been secured yet—that will be done when the deck is installed. At this point, the inside of the hull, where the deck is going, should be smoothed up with a fine rasp.

4. Cut the inwales.

Next, decide how far you want the inwales to extend into the deck; I usually plan on 2" to 2½" (51mm to 64mm). With this established, cut all inwales to the same length to achieve the extension desired. The best way to establish a line that is equal for all four inwales is to measure from the point of the stem, using an equal distance for all of them. Cut the inwales off square for a nice fit into the deck. This is a rather cramped place, so if you have access to a saber saw, you will find this to be the best tool for the job. Otherwise, something like a keyhole saw will have to be used. Whatever you use, be careful not to cut into the side of your canoe.

5. Mark around the inwales.

Once you have established that the deck will fit tightly into the canoe when the notches for the inwales are cut, lay the deck pieces on the canoe and very carefully mark around the ends of the inwales onto the underside of the decks. It is a good idea here to establish which side is up by marking it on the deck. Since you are hand-fitting the deck, it is important that it go in the same way with each fitting. It is important that these lines be accurate to ensure a good fit. When you are ready to cut the notches, stay off your lines (leave a little extra wood) for the final fitting. You can always take a little more off, but you cannot put it back on.

6. Fit the decks.

Fit each deck individually. A helpful hint for achieving a good fit between the deck and the canoe, and a trick of all finish carpenters, is to take a little more wood from the bottom of the deck, where it doesn't show. In other words, taper the edges slightly from top to bottom. This way, minor adjustments are easier to make, and any roughness in the canoe that might interfere with the two pieces coming together evenly with a nice fine line are neutralized.

7. Drill and countersink the screw holes.

When you are satisfied with the fit, establish the locations of the screw holes that will hold the decks in place and the ends of the canoe together. Drill the shank holes in the gunwales and countersink them. Be sure to hold the gunwale in its desired position while drilling the shank holes. You will want one screw through both gunwales where the inwale extends into the notch. These screws will need to be at least 2 inches (51mm) long. The other screws (two more for each side are usually enough) can be 1½" (38mm) long. With both decks fitted and all the shank holes drilled and countersunk, you are ready to install them permanently.

8. Apply glue and screw the decks in place.

Make up some epoxy glue using cotton fibers and a little cedar flour for color. Make the glue stiff enough so it doesn't drip off the mixing stick. It is a good idea to put some papers inside the canoe to protect from any dripping glue. Cover both surfaces with the glue (the deck edges and the inside of the canoe). Extra hands are needed, because you must hold the deck in place and hold the end of the gunwale in place while the pilot hole is drilled and the screws are driven home. If you put in the screw closest to the end first, you can usually relax a little as the other two on that side are driven home. You may want to put some screws on the other side before completing the first side. Your situation will dictate this.

9. Remove excess glue.

When both decks are screwed and glued in place, remove any excess glue that has squeezed out. On the inside, this is best done by taking out gobs of it with a gloved hand. Get it as smooth as possible this way under there, because you will not want, or need, to do any smoothing up later. Remove excess glue on top too, but this area will be dressed down later when the glue has cured.

8a

Apply glue to the decks. Fit the deck and spread a layer of epoxy glue on the deck's edge and on the canoe. Notice the word "top" lightly penciled on the deck. This is to be sure the deck is properly oriented during the hand-fitting process.

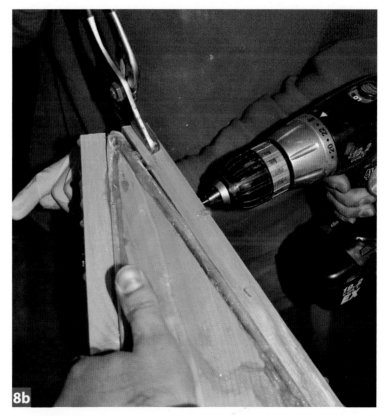

8b

Screw the decks in place. I am using a pair of slip-joint pliers to hold the outside gunwale up in place while Jason drills and drives home a screw. Once the forward screw, the one he is driving, is in place, the gunwale will stay in place by itself as the other screws are driven.

The Decks (continued)

10a

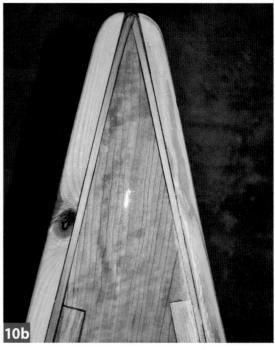

10b

Round off the gunwales. A belt sander is the best tool for dressing down the deck and the gunwales. Keep the sander running with the grain of the wood as much as possible to avoid deep scratches that will have to be removed later.

What a finished gunwale looks like. This photo jumps ahead a little to show the finished deck. That knot on the outside gunwale was the only serious flaw in the nearly 20 foot long strip. We decided that, because it fell in a spot where there would be no stress on it, we would go ahead and use it.

10c

Finish-sand the gunwales. Once you dress down and flush the gunwales and deck, begin the finish sanding. Round off the top of the gunwales a little. It is best to do this sanding with 2 or 3 grits, depending on how much was done with the belt sander. Finish up with 120 grit.

10. Round off the gunwales.

When the glue on the decks has cured, dress them down flush with the gunwales with a belt sander or whatever you have to accomplish this. Once this is done, you should proceed to rounding off the gunwales, inside and out, and smoothing them, along with the decks, with 80-grit and 120-grit sandpaper. It is easier to sand now than when more woodwork is installed.

The Thwarts

Canoes that are 16 feet (4.9 meters) in length or shorter have only one thwart in the center, although you can install more if you wish. For this center thwart in 16 footers, and for the center thwart in longer canoes, I use the yoke shown in the photos and in the patterns. However, suit yourself as to the shape you like for this purpose. The longer canoes should have three thwarts. There is a pattern for the additional thwarts as well. If you wish, you can customize the yoke in the pattern to fit you. The yoke and thwarts can be finished and polyurethaned ahead of time.

The yoke I use, and the one patterned here, is not intended for long portages. It is for the short haul from car to water, etc. When carrying the canoe over long distances, I always tie my paddles in place on the yoke so the canoe rests directly on my shoulders through them. A padding made from my life preserver completes the portage outfit. If one were to make a yoke large enough to be comfortable over a long portage, it would have to be a lot wider than mine, and therefore a lot heavier. You would carry extra weight around day after day just for the occasional use of the heavy yoke. The paddles go with you anyway.

1. Cut and install the yoke.

With the canoe propped to the correct width, lay the yoke across the gunwales so that its center is in exactly the center of the canoe. Now you should decide which end of the canoe will be the bow—face the yoke (opening for the neck) in that direction. Next, take a straightedge and lay it across the yoke, lining it up with the outside of the canoe hull. Mark along the straightedge. This would seem to make the yoke too long, but with the curve of the canoe, it will come out just about right. Without disturbing the yoke, make a similar mark on its other end. Cut the yoke at your marks, and it is ready to install. With the yoke held up against the underside of the inwale, drill and countersink two holes for a 2" (51mm), 10-24 flathead machine screw. Tighten the machine screws with a washer and nut underneath.

Cut and install the yoke. Mount the yoke and thwarts with 2" (51mm), 10-24 flathead machine bolts, along with nuts and washers. Use two bolts on the yoke as seen here and one on the thwarts. In this case, these pieces were pre-finished, but you can do them with the rest of the canoe if you wish.

2. Install the thwarts.

If yours is a longer canoe, the other two thwarts are installed in a similar manner, except only one machine screw is needed. Where you place these two thwarts along the length of the canoe will vary with the length. A good rule of thumb is to decide where the front seat will go (allowing leg-room for the bow person) and install one of the thwarts two or three inches (51 or 76mm) behind the seat. Install the other thwart the same distance from the yoke as the first.

The Seats

If your seats are ready, or at least the uncaned frames, it is a good idea to install them now and then remove them before varnishing the canoe and woodwork. If you wish to do this, skip to the end of the seat chapter and install them according to the directions there.

Bolt the seat in place. Jason's thumb is over the spacer. Remove the seats after the fitting is complete to facilitate the finish coating of polyurethane on the hull and the woodwork. Re-install the seats after the finish is complete and dry.

Mount the seats before you finish the canoe. If you have them ready, it is a good idea to mount the seats before starting the finishing on the canoe. Drill a large hole deep enough to countersink the head of the carriage bolt and then drill the rest of the way through the inside gunwale. Make up spacers by drilling a hole through it. These go between the seat and the underside of the gunwale.

Finishing Up

1. Install low-line attachment holes.

Depending on how you plan to use your canoe, you may want to consider installing the low-line attachment holes shown in the photos at right. These allow you to line your canoe through rapids without the danger of pulling sideways and possibly causing an upset. They are also beneficial if you ever have to tow the canoe.

To install the low-line attachment, cut two pieces of ¾" (19mm) copper tubing 2" (51mm) long. Next, locate where you want the line to attach. Usually, this would be just about the average waterline. Drill a hole through the canoe just slightly larger than the outside of the tubing. Using sandpaper, scratch up the surface of the tubing to give the epoxy a surface to "grab" onto. Mix up some epoxy and thicken with silica and cedar flour. Coat the outside of the tubing and the inside of the hole in the canoe. Insert the tubing and allow to cure for at least 24 hours. Trim the ends of the tubing as close to flush with the canoe hull as possible and then sand it flush.

1a **1b**

Install a low-line attachment hole. A low rope attachment has an advantage in towing or lining a canoe through a difficult set of rapids. Simply drill a hole large enough for a piece of ¾" copper tubing and fit the tubing in with some epoxy glue. When the glue has cured, cut off the tubing and dress it down flush with the hull.

Finishing Up (continued)

Add rope. If you keep a bow and stern line on your canoe (as you should), here is a good way to stow them so they will not get tangled up with your feet. And, they are always readily available when needed. A couple of holes in the deck and a short length of shock cord are all that is needed.

Coat the gunwales with polyurethane. While the inside of the hull is drying after a thorough wash down, coat the gunwales with polyurethane. The following day, coat the inside of the hull and apply another coat on the woodwork. Repeat these coats again. Thus, you'll have two coats on the inside of the hull and three coats on the woodwork.

2. Apply polyurethane.

With the woodwork all installed and sanded smooth, you are ready to move on and give your canoe at least two coats of a good exterior polyurethane with an ultraviolet filter. The Zar brand is a good choice. Before you start out putting on the finish coat, be sure you thoroughly wash down the hull with clean water to remove any traces of the dust remaining from your final sanding of the hull. If you fail to do this, you risk a gummy coating of poly that will not cure. I learned this lesson the hard way! With the hull thoroughly cleaned, use a rag dampened with paint thinner to wipe down the woodwork. When the hull is thoroughly dry, go ahead and apply the poly.

Coat the outside of the hull. Apply two coats of polyurethane just like the inside. If you get scratches on the hull in the future, give them a light sanding and then a coating of poly.

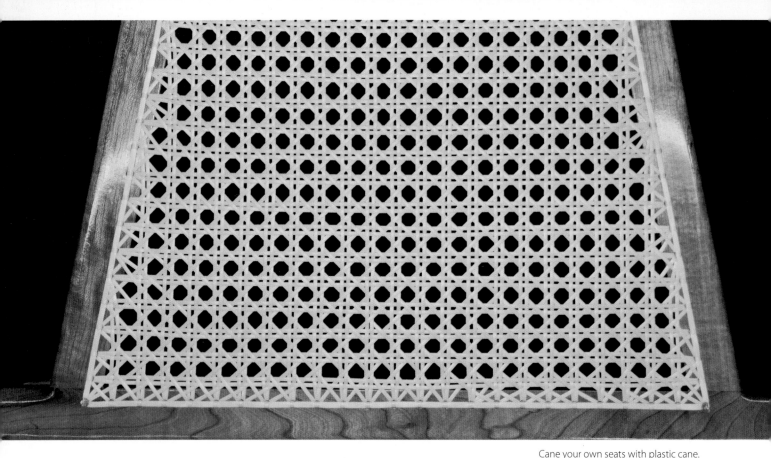

Cane your own seats with plastic cane. Your body will thank you!

Chapter 7

Seats

In his book *Maine Lingo*, Maine humorist John Gould gives the following regional interpretation of an otherwise common English word:

Ample – Favored Maine word to express satisfaction at the table:

"Have more potatoes, Cyrus?"

"No thanks Helen, ample of everything."

A time-tested dialogue as old as Maine is between a deaf hostess and her gentleman guest. She speaks first:

More vegetables, Jonathan?

No, thanks—great sufficiency.

Been a-fishin'?

No, I say—I've got plenty!

Caught twenty?

No, no—I'm full!

Broke your pole?

No, no, ample, ample!

Small sample—pass up your plate!

In my section of Maine the word was also used, especially by my grandparents' generation, to describe something as being large enough that its size could be put out of mind for once and for all. My grandparents might be heard to say:

"That crock big enough, Ben?"

"Ample, Gertie, ample."

The reason for this bit of northern New England humor is simply so that you will know what I mean when I describe my canoe seats as ample. They are big enough so a person can spend the day on one of them and have room to squirm, wiggle, and shift to stay comfortable. Furthermore, the plastic cane has enough stretch and ventilation to make the above contortions all but unnecessary. Never, after a day on the canoe, did I feel the urge to stand and rub my posterior to restore circulation. Since most of my summer days were spent in the seat of a canoe, I valued this bit of comfort, and so I do not skimp on the seats. It takes only a little extra care to make a first-class seat. I can't for the life of me understand why some canoe builders insist on putting in seats that are little better to sit on than a thwart!

Making the Frames

The hardwood for the seats can be ¾" (19mm) or thicker. If you think you need a stronger seat for whatever reason, the additional material can come from the additional thickness or from additional width of your hardwood stock. Do whichever is easier for you with the tools and material you have to work with. I have found ¾" x 1½" (19mm x 38mm) material to be adequate for most uses. If you need to beef up your seat either with thickness or width, you can make the adjustments to the instructions as needed. The instructions in this chapter will be based on material sawn to ¾" x 1½" (19mm x 38mm). As for the kind of hardwood, as long as it is one of the stronger ones, like ash, oak, maple, cherry, or birch, the seats will be strong enough.

1. Cut the hardwood for the seats.

Rip up enough hardwood stock to make the front, back, and sides of your seats. The front and back will have to be long enough to reach from gunwale to gunwale at the point in your canoe or boat where you will mount it. The sides will need to be 13⁵⁄₁₆" (338mm) when finished. For now, cut all four pieces to length plus about one inch (1" [25mm] longer than finished length). The front and back of the bow seat should be 32" and 36" (813mm and 914mm). For the stern seat, make them 17" and 21" (432mm and 533mm). The front and back will be oversized; you cut to final length when the seat is installed in the canoe.

2. Mark the tenons.

Take a look at **Figure 7-1**, and you will see that the seat sides need to be cut at an angle of 12°, and the overall length of the pieces should be 13⁵⁄₁₆" (338mm). Make these measurements and cuts carefully, as they determine the angle of entry of your tenons into the mortises, which you will cut in the front and back pieces. The tenon length will be ½" (13mm), so measure from both ends back ½" (13mm) and mark for the tenon. You should make the tenon marks completely around the piece (top, bottom, and both edges)—that way you will have a guide to cut by no matter which way you turn the piece or how you make the cuts.

Materials and tools needed to make and mount the seats

Materials:	Tools:
■ Hardwood stock, ¾" x 1½" (19mm x 38mm), 15 feet long (4.5 meters)	■ Table saw
■ Epoxy and cotton fibers for glue	■ Power drill/driver
	■ Power sander
■ Sandpaper, 80 and 120 grits	■ Level
■ Polyurethane	■ Rule
■ Medium cane, 1 roll or hank with binder	■ Handsaw
■ Carriage bolts, ¼" (6mm); two 6" (152mm), six 4" (102mm) with nuts and washers	■ ⁵⁄₁₆" (8mm) drill bit
	■ ½" or ⁵⁄₈" (13mm or 16mm) drill bit
■ Dowels or scrap hardwood to make spacers for installing seats	■ Hammer
	■ Knife
■ Petroleum jelly (optional)	■ Awl or nail
	■ 12 (or more) pegs for caning

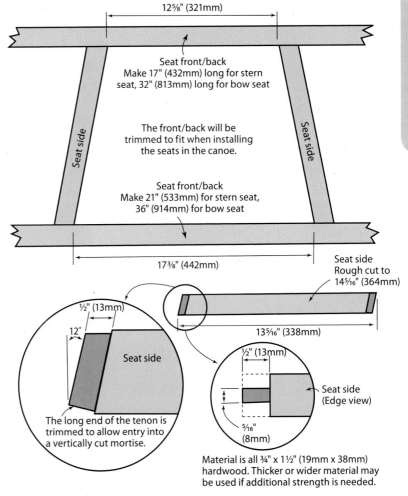

This is a suggested shape. Any reasonable shape can be made and caned.

12⁵⁄₈" (321mm)

Seat front/back
Make 17" (432mm) long for stern seat, 32" (813mm) long for bow seat

Seat side

Seat side

The front/back will be trimmed to fit when installing the seats in the canoe.

Seat front/back
Make 21" (533mm) for stern seat, 36" (914mm) for bow seat

17⅜" (442mm)

Seat side
Rough cut to 14⁵⁄₁₆" (364mm)

½" (13mm)

12°

Seat side

The long end of the tenon is trimmed to allow entry into a vertically cut mortise.

13⁵⁄₁₆" (338mm)

½" (13mm)

Seat side
(Edge view)

⁵⁄₁₆" (8mm)

Material is all ¾" x 1½" (19mm x 38mm) hardwood. Thicker or wider material may be used if additional strength is needed.

Figure 7-1: Canoe seat dimensions. These are suggested dimensions for an "ample" canoe seat. The mortise and tenon joint is the strongest wood joint in the woodworker's repertoire. So, combine this joint with epoxy glue and you have an unbeatable combination.

3. Mark the mortises.

Following the dimensions in Figure 7-1, mark the locations of the mortises in the front and back pieces. These mortises should each be made 1⅜" (35mm) long, or ⅛" (3mm) shorter than the width of the pieces being joined. See also the tenon detail. By making the joint slightly smaller than the parts, there will be no evidence of the joint on the finished seat. Or, to put it another way, you won't be able to see the ends of the mortises.

The mortise and tenon joint is the strongest wood joint in the woodworker's repertoire. So, combine this joint with epoxy glue and you have an unbeatable combination. Of course, you should always strive for a good wood to wood fit whenever you make a joint, but if you should make a mistake, the gap filling properties of the cotton fiber/epoxy mix will bail you out and save a lot of wood in the process.

4. Cut the tenons.

Carefully cut the tenons with a back-saw or other fine-toothed saw. A jig can be constructed to hold the parts at the correct angle, allowing you to make your cuts on a band saw, but for a few cuts it is hardly worth the effort. The tenons can be made on a table saw with the miter set at the proper angle and the blade at the proper height.

Notice in the detail of Figure 7-1 that the tenon is cut slightly smaller (1/16" [2mm]) than the side of the seat. Also, the long side is trimmed so as to enter a vertically cut mortise. This trimming is unnecessary if you wish to cut the mortise at the proper angle, but usually it is easier to make it at a right angle to the surface, especially if you do it with power equipment.

5. Cut the mortises.

The simplest way to cut the mortises is with a ¼" (6mm) wood chisel and a hammer. If you have a power hand drill, you can save time by drilling inside your lines and then cleaning out what remains with the chisel. If you have a drill press, the whole job can be done on it with a 5/16" (8mm) router bit. The depth of the mortises should be a little deeper than the length of the tenons to ensure they will not bottom-out. Make them at least 9/16" (14mm) deep—⅝" (16mm) would even be OK.

6. Fit the joints together.

When both parts of the joints are cut, go ahead and fit them together. This will usually require some hand work with a fine rasp to make the tenon slide snugly into the mortise. If you made the mortises with a router bit on the drill press, the ends of the openings are rounded. It is easier to round off the ends of the tenons to match these openings than to square off the mortises. Either is OK, however.

7. Glue the joints.

When you are satisfied that all joints come together properly, glue them together with your epoxy glue. Put enough thickened mixture into the mortises that you are sure the cavity will be completely filled with the tenon and the glue. When the four joints are assembled, clamp together with bar clamps. Lacking bar clamps, a twisted rope between the front and back pieces will hold them firmly together until the final cure is reached. You may also be able to stand the seat on edge and place weight on top to hold things in place. At any rate, the joints should remain stationary until the final cure is reached (24 hours).

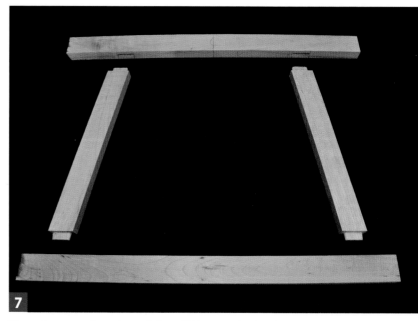

7

The seat parts ready to glue and clamp. With epoxy glue, it isn't necessary to exert a lot of clamping pressure, so a make-do method can be devised if bar clamps are not available.

8. Smooth the joints.

When the clamps are removed, you should smooth up the joints with a sander. Next, round off the outside of the seat either with a router and rounding cutter or by hand with a rasp, and then go ahead and do the rough sanding with 60 grit.

9. Locate the corner holes.

Before you do any further smoothing it is a good idea to mark and drill the holes for the caning. The completed holes can be seen in the photo on page 78. The holes will be ¼" (6mm) in diameter and will be ¾" (19mm) apart on a line ⅜" (10mm) from the inside edge of the seat. The first thing to do is to measure out ⅜" (10mm) from the inside edge and draw a line on all four sides. Where these lines meet at the corners there will be a corner hole.

10. Mark the caning holes.

Next, find the center of each of the four sides and a mark it on the ⅜" (10mm) line. Now, measuring out toward the corners from that center mark, make a mark every ¾" (19mm) until you reach the corner. Since there will be a hole in each corner, you may have to fudge the last couple of marks before reaching the corner; they won't necessarily come out even. You can either make them a little closer than ¾" (19mm) or a little further apart, depending on the adjustment needed. The change of spacing will not be noticeable in the completed seat. Since you are starting from the center, whatever adjustment you make at one end of the side, you will make the same adjustment at the other. And, whatever adjustment you make on one side, you should do the same on the opposing side.

11. Drill the holes.

When you are satisfied with your marks, go ahead and drill the holes using a ¼" (6mm) drill bit. A drill press does the best job, but careful aligning with a power hand drill will do almost as well.

Other Joints

The mortise and tenon joint is not the only choice for assembling the seats, although it is my preference and has stood the test of time on my canoes. A lap joint or doweled joint could be used if you prefer.

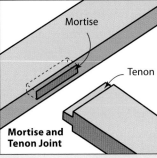

Mortise

Tenon

Mortise and Tenon Joint

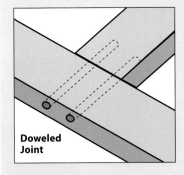

Doweled Joint

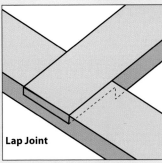

Lap Joint

Other joints. There are a few wood joints that can be used to make seats. The one on top, mortise and tenon, is the strongest and preferred. The doweled joint is easy to make, but its strength depends on the strength of the dowels. The lap joint is probably the weakest, as you are cutting halfway through one of the members of the seat.

Rectangular Seat

You can make a very satisfactory seat by joining the parts at right angles rather than the angles of the seat sides in Figure 7-1. That seat was designed to follow the lines of the canoe gunwales, and looks good when installed. A strictly rectangular seat saves you the problem of careful cutting of angles and fitting them into the mortises. Tenons for rectangular seats can be easily cut with power equipment, whereas it is often easier to cut the angled tenons by hand than to set up power equipment for such a few cuts. If you decide on rectangular seats, then ignore the reference to angles in the following paragraphs and simply join yours at 90°.

Making the Frames (continued)

12. Finish the wooden parts of the seat.
When the holes are all drilled, you can do the final sanding and coat your seat with polyurethane. Since you will probably do your caning with plastic cane (highly recommended for outside applications), which needs no finish, you will want the wooden parts completely finished before starting the caning process.

Now give the caning section a quick read and you will see that caning is not as scary as you may have thought.

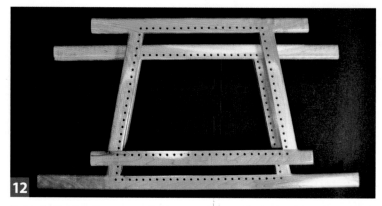

Finish the front and rear seats. Finish seats to be caned beforehand, because no finish is needed for the plastic cane. A couple of coats of exterior polyurethane bring out the color of these cherry wood seats.

Caning

Years ago, in an adult canoe building class, one of my students who had experience caning chair seats with natural cane remarked that he was going to do his canoe seats with the real thing. I asked him why. He replied that he liked the idea of using traditional materials, the modern plastic seeming somehow out of place. I laughed and pointed out that he was using space-age materials to build his canoe, even though the finished product did have a natural appearance. He laughed along with me and replied that he had not thought of it in that way. Since the students caned their seats at home, I never learned which he ended up using.

Natural cane has one disadvantage that makes it unsuitable for canoe seats, in my opinion. It stretches and sags in damp weather, and then it does not return to its original shape when dry. The plastic cane always remains taut and flexible, bounces back from the roughest treatment, and seems to be unaffected by heat and cold. I have plastic caned canoe seats that have been in use for so long, I'm beginning to think the cane will outlast the wooden frame it is strung upon.

If you have prepared for the caning operation, you should already have the necessary tools and materials to complete this important phase of the seat project. The photo at top right shows the items you will need for weaving plastic cane, and I will explain the purpose of each item as we get to it.

Caning supplies. At the top is a jar of petroleum jelly. The hammer has limited use, but you will need it eventually. The purpose of the knife is obvious. Make from dowels, or buy, a good supply (at least a dozen) of hardwood pegs. Your cane may look different, but the large roll is medium cane and the small bundle is binder cane.

From time to time cane comes in different-looking spools and hanks, so yours might differ from the cane and binder in the photo. Vaseline is shown for a lubricating agent for the cane when you pull it through. The friction of the cane sliding between layers of cane can melt the plastic, so lubrication is necessary. I included the Vaseline because that is what the "experts" recommend. I personally just dip my fingers into a container of water and coat the cane with it before pulling through. It works fine, and I never had a melted cane! The Vaseline picks up a lot of dirt as you work—the water is a lot less messy.

Caning (continued)

1. Clamp the seat.

Get comfortable, and we'll get to work. I will be referring to the back and front of the seat from time to time, so let's establish which is which for our purposes. We will consider the wide part of the seat (closest to you) the front, and the narrow part the back. The two angled pieces in the photos will be called the sides. If your seat is of a different design, just establish the front from the back and be consistent. Some work with the seat in their lap, but I prefer to have it sturdily clamped in place at a convenient working height. Work out whatever works best for you.

2. Measure the cane.

Start out by counting the holes in the front and back to find the center hole of each, which you then mark with a peg. Get out a convenient length of cane. Somewhere around 12 feet (3.6 meters) works well. Use your arms as a convenient measure. Most people can reach roughly their own height with their arms outstretched.

Clamp the seat. Clamping the seat to the edge of a bench or table is a good way to secure them for caning. Free access to the top and bottom of the seat is necessary for efficient caning.

Insert pegs into holes as you go in order to keep the cane tight.

Caning (continued)

3. String up and down.

Start in the rear center hole and string the cane across to the front center hole. Notice that the cane has a right side and a wrong side. The rounded side should be up; you will have to keep it that way throughout the project. Be sure to leave 4 or 5 inches (102 to 127mm) of cane hanging below the seat wherever there is an end so that you will have something to get ahold of when you tie off later. You will go down through the front center hole and come up through the one to its right. Go across toward the rear and go down through the hole to the right of the rear center hole. Continue stringing the cane this way until the side is filled like the photo on page 79. Follow along with a peg from hole to hole to hold the cane tight as you work. You don't have to pull the cane really tight, but just enough to keep the strands straight and in place. Things will tighten up later when you begin to weave.

When you approach the angled sides, just keep the shorter strands parallel with the others by moving from hole to hole along the angled pieces. The shorter strands on each side may have to be pegged on both ends so that the cane will not be strung across the holes underneath the seat. When you have filled in the right side of the seat, string up the other side in the same manner.

4. String side to side.

Start this step by pegging off the end of your strand in the hole next to the right rear corner. Go across the seat horizontally to the corresponding hole on the other side. You are stringing these strands right over those put on in the previous step. Continue stringing horizontally across your seat until it is filled from rear to front. Don't worry about all those untied strands hanging below the seat; we'll get to them shortly.

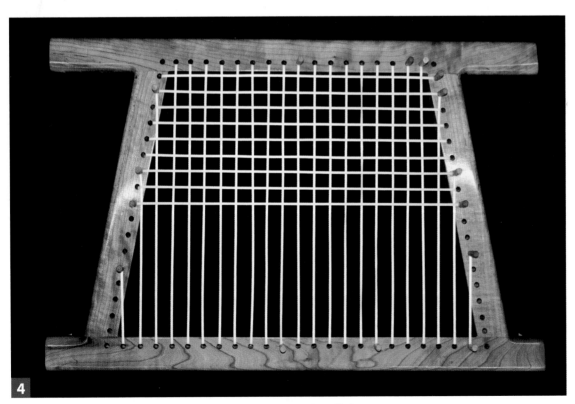

4

String horizontally. Continue stringing horizontally across your seat until it is filled from rear to front.

5. String up and down again.

So far, things are easy. They aren't going to get much more complicated either. This step is a repetition of Step 3. Start in a hole on one side or the other of the one you started in with Step 3, and string a new vertical layer of cane right over the layers put on in Steps 3 and 4. You'll end up with three layers of cane. The photo shows the right side of the seat with this step completed. I tried to push the strands apart a little so you could see the three layers.

6. Tie off the loose ends.

There are now a lot pegs in the holes. Since they have to be removed and replaced when doing succeeding steps, it is a good idea to minimize them whenever possible. When your seat looks like this one, turn it over, and we'll do something about some of those loose ends and also get rid of some of the pegs at the same time.

This is the simple method of tying off the loose ends. It doesn't look too secure, but don't worry— the ties will stay in place. At the present time, you can only tie off the ends that have a loop next to them; those that don't are left until later. Take a look at the photo below for a visual on tying the knots. You want to thread the cane under the closest loop and then through the loop that creates.

I think neatness counts here. You may have noticed that the difference between professional and amateur work in any field is usually how the parts are finished that do not normally show. Your first seat can look like a pro's if you take a little care in tying off. Keep the ends all pointing in the same direction and cut them all the same length. I think it looks best if the ends are pointing in and are cut off at ⅛" (3mm) from the inside edge. You can remove all the pegs where you managed to tie off; leave the rest until you have a loop to tie them to. From now on, tie off what you can after completing each step.

5a

String up and down again. String a new vertical layer of cane right over the layers put on in Steps 3 and 4.

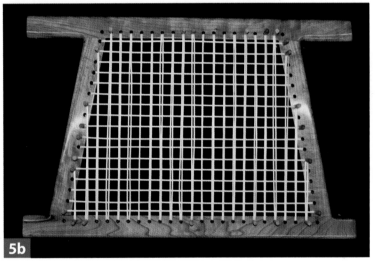

5b

Complete the new vertical layer.

6

Tie-off the loose ends. Don't be deceived—this tying-off method doesn't look too secure, but it works.

Caning (continued)

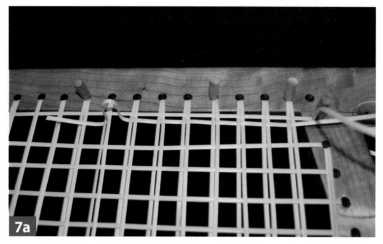

7a

Weave over the top canes and under the bottom canes.

7b

Keep weaving. This photo shows that when you reach the left side and start back across, the weaving pattern looks identical to that of the first strand.

7. Begin weaving.

Now you start weaving for the first time. You start this step in the same hole as you used to begin Step 4. Study the photo carefully. You will weave over the top canes and under the bottom canes, in that order. It is important that you keep the cane right side up, because if it twists as you pull it through, you'll probably have to take it out to straighten the strand. There isn't too much friction at this stage of the weaving, but it is a good idea to start lubricating the strands before you pull them through. Use water or petroleum jelly. You can weave all the way across before pulling the rest of the cane through if it is properly lubricated. Go down through the hole corresponding to the one you started with. Push the woven squares tightly together as you complete a strand. If you, like me, keep yourself weaving correctly when going from right to left by repeating, "over the top, under the bottom," then when you start going from left to right, reverse the phrase and say: "under the bottom, over the top." Same weave, different order.

Be conscientious about keeping the under-and-over weave consistent; it will prevent confusion and a lot of pulling out when you make the diagonal weaves in the following steps. Notice how the woven squares are pulled together and how they form a larger square hole in the woven pattern (see photo at bottom). Tie off wherever you can and you are ready to proceed to the diagonal weaving.

Complete the horizontal weave. Notice how the woven squares form a larger square hole in the woven pattern now that Step 7 is complete.

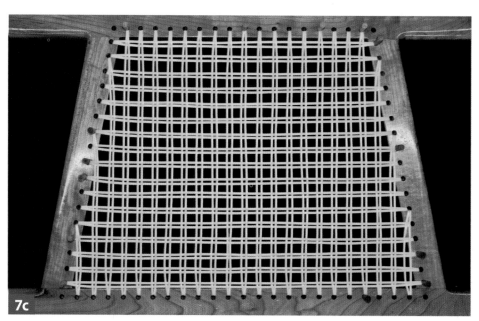

7c

8. Weave diagonally from right to left.

Now the fun begins—making the diagonal weaves that complete the pattern. The first diagonal starts in the right rear corner and weaves under the pairs running from side to side and over the pairs running from front to rear. The photo at right shows the beginning of this step.

If you happened to reverse things in Step 7 (went under where you should have gone over, etc) you can save pulling it all out by reversing this step and Step 9. Give the cane a little tug at the end of the weave just to ensure a good tight weave.

As you do your diagonal weaving, you will find that it is necessary to either skip a hole in the frame or to double up on one from time to time to preserve the spacing of the weave. Look closely at the photo at bottom and you will see where I doubled up on the side and skipped on the front. Also, notice that there are two canes coming from both corner holes. In the trade this is called a "Bird's Head," and it makes your job look really professional. Tie off where you can and move on to Step 9. Don't worry about tying off the corner holes. Leave the pegs there; we'll finish up the corners a little later.

8a

Weave diagonally from right to left. The first diagonal starts in the right rear corner.

8b

Keep the diagonal weave straight. This photo shows how to ensure you have your weave right. The peg points to where the diagonal can easily slip between the horizontal and vertical canes. If you have it wrong, the diagonal will take on a snake-like look instead of being straight like the ones in this photo.

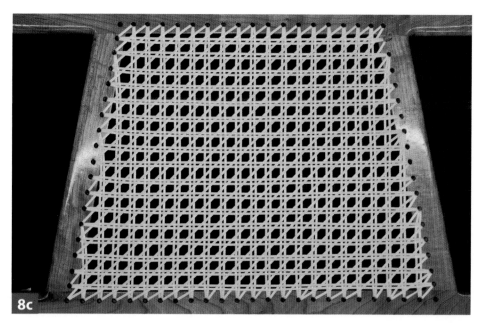

8c

Double up when needed. Look close to see where I doubled up some diagonal weaving on the side and skipped some on the front. Sometimes it is necessary to do this to maintain the spacing of the weave.

Caning (continued)

9a

Weave diagonally from left to right. Weave over the pairs running from side to side and under the pairs running from front to rear.

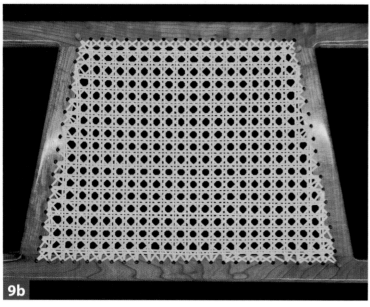

9b

The weaving is complete. Notice a nice "Bird's Head" in each corner. A close inspection will show those places where the cane was doubled up in a hole or a hole was skipped.

9. Weave diagonally from left to right.

This step starts in the left rear corner and makes just the opposite diagonal weave of the sequence in Step 8. You will weave over the pairs running from side to side and under the pairs running from front to rear. It is increasingly important that you keep the canes lubricated as you pull them through, because the weave is getting tighter and tighter. If using water, keep your fingers wet as you pull the cane through them. About now you may be having a little trouble getting the cane up and down through the holes as they fill up with cane. There's plenty of room—you just have to push things around a little to open up the hole. Use a nail, an awl, or something similar to do this.

You can see in the photo at bottom left that there are now "Bird's Heads" in each corner. There are also a few skipped and doubled-up holes—but the important thing is to keep the cane running as straight as possible. When it is necessary to have the cane "lean" in one direction (because going straight there is no hole), make them lean as these in the photo do. It makes a better-looking job.

10. Cut the binder.

This step is called the binder, and is the finishing touch to your caning job. The binder cane is sometimes included with the medium cane, and sometimes you have to order it separately. Be sure to get it one way or another. The binder is wider than the weaving cane and its purpose is to cover up the holes around the edge of your seat. If, for some reason, you failed to get wide binder cane, then go ahead and use the medium cane; it is better than no binder at all.

Start by cutting a length of binder cane a couple of inches longer than the distance between the corner holes on the side you are starting first. Pull it tight and peg both ends into the corners.

11. Apply the binder.

With a piece of medium cane about 3 feet (1 meter) long, go up and down through the hole nearest one corner, around the binder. Leave enough hanging below to tie off later. Snug the medium cane down over the binder cane as shown in the photo. Move on and go up and down through the next hole. Repeat this until you use up the medium cane. Cut a new piece and continue until you have been all the way around the seat. When you have completed the binding, you should be able to tie off all loose ends hanging below the seat except the corners.

12. Drive in softwood pegs.

You should have a peg in each corner. If the pegs are made of hardwood (remember that most dowels are hardwood), replace them with pegs made of a soft wood such as cedar. You are finally going to use that hammer. Drive the softwood pegs securely into the holes, score them with a knife even with the seat surface, and break them off. If a little roughness persists, tap it with the hammer to smooth it out.

Any cane hanging below the lower surface of the seat at the corners can be trimmed flush with the surface. The seat is now complete!

11

Add the binder. This is the finishing touch that covers the holes around the border.

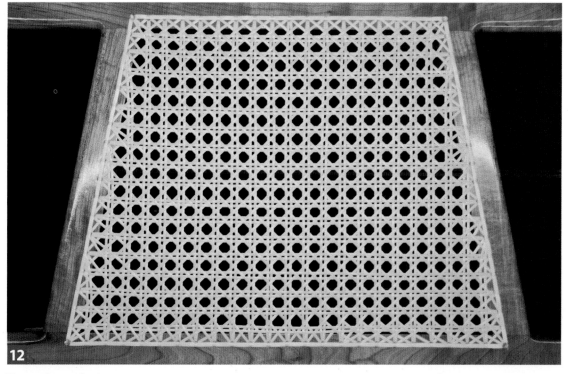

12

The seat is complete!

Installing the Seats

1. Trim the seats to fit.

As mentioned earlier, the lengths of the front/rear pieces of the seats are left long so they can be trimmed to fit any canoe when you are ready to install them. First, position the seats. The rear seat should be as far to the rear of the canoe as you can get it, so you will trim off the rear (short) horizontal piece right down to the frame itself. The amount trimmed from the front of the stern seat will depend on the canoe shape. This is best done by the trial and error system. Take a little off each end repeatedly until the rear of the seat touches the sides of the hull and the front crosspiece does as well.

2. Position the seats.

The position of the bow seat can vary according to individual taste and need (and leg length of the bow person), but a good starting point is 40 to 45 inches (1,016mm to 1,143mm) from the point of the stem. The tapered seat should be installed so the sides are parallel with the sides of the canoe.

3. Make spacers.

The seats are hung from the gunwales with ¼" (6mm) carriage bolts. You will need two 6" (152mm) bolts and six 4" (102mm) bolts along with nuts and washers. Drill out the centers of dowels with a 5⁄16" (8mm) bit to place over the bolts and between the seat and the gunwale. Pieces of sawed off gunwale strips were used for this in the photos. Make two of these spacers 4" (102mm) long and six of them 2½" (64mm) long. You will trim them to exact fit later.

4. Drill holes.

Line up the seats in the desired positions and mark the top of the gunwale where you will drill. First drill a countersink hole large enough to accommodate the head of the carriage bolt. Drill this only deep enough to sink the bolt's head below the surface of the gunwale. Next drill 5⁄16" (8mm) holes through the gunwale. Drop the carriage bolts through the holes and, while holding the seats in position, mark the spot where the bolt is to go through the seat. Drill the seats with a 5⁄16" (8mm) drill bit.

5. Attach the seats.

Put the bolts through the gunwales and the seat, and turn on the nuts with the washers. With the canoe sitting on a level surface, use a level and level the seats by turning the nuts. When the seats are level, measure and cut the spacers to the exact fit and angle of the gunwale. Remove the seats and remount them with the bolts and spacers in place. Tighten the nuts to secure the seats in place. Study the photos at right and the above explanation will mostly be self-evident.

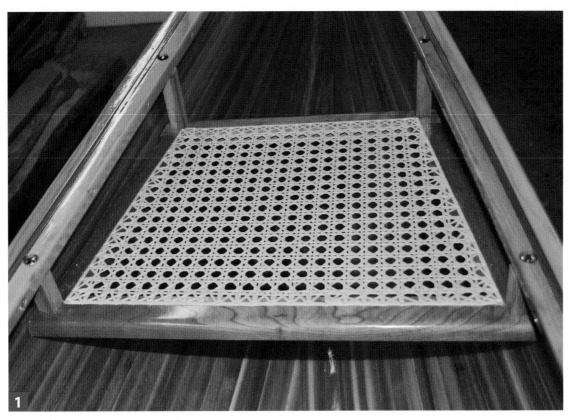

The rear seat has been installed.

The front seat has been installed.

Chapter 8

Repairs

Inevitably, you will need to make a repair to your canoe. But don't worry! It's not any more difficult than the original work you did with fiberglass.

I was on the stream near our home in my 16-foot (4.9-meter) Wabnaki. Recent rains had raised the water level and the whitewater portion of the trip was proving to be exciting and enjoyable. I have canoed the stream countless times, so I knew what to expect, but every water level offers up its unique challenges. I aligned the canoe with the chute through the drop ahead and I knew that the stream made a sharp turn to the right as soon as I reached the bottom of the drop. As soon as I cleared the chute, I did a hard draw to the right to get around the bend in the stream. The current was too strong, and in spite of my efforts, my canoe was swept toward the left bank of the stream. Before I could correct the drift, the stern of the canoe smacked into a rock—a very sharp rock as it turned out.

I heard the crunch and knew there was some damage, but since it was above the waterline, and I could see no damage to the inside of the canoe, I continued without further incident. When I reached my take-out, I inspected the damage and knew I had a repair to make before the canoe was put away. The repair process is shown in the photos in this chapter.

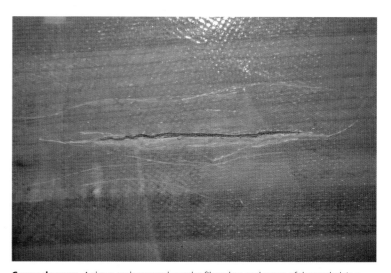

Canoe damage. A sharp rock gouged out the fiberglass and some of the underlying cedar. This kind of damage is kind of rare, and usually happens below the waterline.

Damages

Fiberglassed strip canoes are tough, but they have their limits. If you use your canoe extensively, you will eventually learn what those limits are. In my guiding business, I put 500 to 700 miles (800 to 1125 kilometers) of water travel per season on my personal 20-foot (6.1-meter) White Guide Model—about half of it on rivers, which by the end of the season were often very shallow. At times, I would find myself more concerned with the welfare and progress of my guests than I was with guiding my own canoe. The result was often a collision with a barely submerged rock. Most of the time, the canoe slid over the offending rock and there was nothing more than a scratch on the bottom of the canoe. Sometimes the rock was too much for the heavily laden canoe and more serious damage would result.

I never had damage to a strip canoe that allowed water to come pouring into the canoe. The damage was a break in the exterior fiberglass, which would go unnoticed until the end of the day when the canoe was turned over. A temporary repair would then be made with duct tape and the problem forgotten until we returned home. At times, a break would go unnoticed for several days. This, of course, allowed more water to soak into the cedar strips between the two layers of fiberglass.

It is not uncommon for damages to a canoe to happen on dry land, far from the canoe's native element. I described previously the canoe that was blown off my truck and tumbled end over end down the road. A canoe left unsecured where the wind can pick it up can also be damaged. A canoe has a lot of surface area compared to its weight. I left a canoe out behind my house for a day and it was picked up by the wind and deposited squarely on the casing of our well. It made a dandy hole!

I hope these descriptions of damaged strip canoes do not discourage you. The canoes really are tough, but accidents do happen. If you know you will use your canoe in whitewater and/or shallow rocky rivers, you should consider an extra layer of fiberglass on the bottom or a football-shaped piece of Kevlar. These are discussed in the Fiberglassing chapter (page 39). These reinforcing layers are more easily done during the construction of the canoe, but a retrofit is readily accomplished and will serve just as well.

Materials and tools needed to make repairs

- Fiberglass fabric (scraps left over from the canoe construction)
- Small amount of resin and hardener
- Sandpaper, 80 and 120 grit

Tools:

- Scissors
- Tool to cut away the damaged fiberglass (could use a wood chisel or a power carver)
- Power sander
- Disposable brushes for wetting out patch(es) and applying fill coats
- Containers for resin
- Protective eyewear
- Dust mask(s)
- Disposable gloves

Repairing Outside Damage

1. Expose the wet wood.

When it is time to make repairs, the fiberglass is cut away like that shown in the photo at left. I use a Dremel tool with a round bit, but a chisel will do the job too. A below-waterline break results in soaked wood, so the size of the opening must be enlarged until dry wood is reached. The wood should be left exposed until thoroughly dry. Applying heat from a lamp or a small electric heater can speed up the drying process.

The danger of water-soaked wood below the fiberglass is delamination. However, because of the tenacious grip the epoxy has on the wood, the delamination is mostly of the wood fibers separating, not the fiberglass. When the fiberglass is peeled away, wood fibers are still clinging to the inside surface. This leaves a rough surface in the wood that will require some sanding, and/or in some cases filling, before the fiberglass patches are applied. The longer the below-waterline break is exposed to water, the larger the wetted wood will become, thus requiring a larger patch.

Expose the wet wood. For this repair, I could have just filled the cavity and put a piece of fiberglass on the surface, but I wanted to show the steps needed to make a repair when there is water in the wood. Enlarge the opening until dry wood is reached.

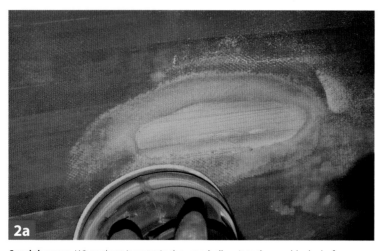

Sand the area. When there is water in the wood, allow it to thoroughly dry before proceeding. Then sand to feather the edge opening in the fiberglass and remove varnish out to about 2" (51mm) all the way around to provide a good mechanical bond for the large patch you are going to apply.

2. Sand and fill the damaged area.

Once the wood has dried out, you can proceed with the sanding and filling. If the wood is rough and/or gouged, then fill to provide a smooth surface. At the same time, feather the edges of the fiberglass around the opening. Sand away the old varnish a couple of inches around the opening to provide a surface for a good mechanical bond. If you had to fill some gouges in the wood, you do not have to wait for the filler to cure. Just go ahead and start the patching.

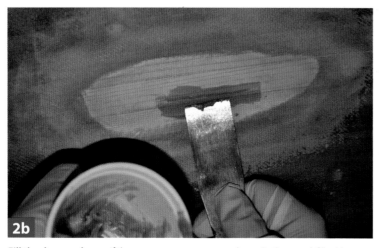

Fill the damaged area. If there are any gouges or roughness in the wood, fill with an epoxy, silica, and cedar flour mixture. Add just enough cedar flour to get a close match to the wood color. You do not have to wait for the filler mixture to cure before proceeding.

New layer of resin?

I have had folks ask about coating the entire hull with a new layer of resin. The patch they did looked so bright and new they wanted the whole canoe to look that way. This is a bad idea. The resin adds more weight and you still have to sand it down and coat with polyurethane. Better to just omit the resin, sand, and apply a new coat of polyurethane.

3. Cut patches of fiberglass.

Cut one or more patches of fiberglass the same size as the opening you created. The number of patches used for this depends on how thick the original fiberglass was. Cut another patch about 1½ to 2" (38 to 51mm) larger than the opening. Mix up a small amount of resin and wet out the small patch(es).

4. Apply the larger patch.

Proceed to apply the larger patch, which will extend out to the area sanded for that purpose. Unless your patches are enormous, you will not need a squeegee or a roller for the patching. A disposable brush will do just fine. If necessary, follow up with a filler coat of resin to completely fill the weave of the cloth.

Wet out the small patch(es). Use plenty of resin. The masking tape and wax paper shown below the repair are to catch drips and so avoid having to sand them off later. Do all of the epoxy work with a disposable brush.

Apply the larger patch. Immediately place the larger patch over the smaller ones and wet it out. If you are working on a fairly level surface, you may be able to apply enough resin at this time to avoid applying a filler coat. If not, allow the patch to reach the gel stage and apply the filler coat.

Repairing Outside Damage (continued)

5. Sand the patch.

When all is cured, 24 or more hours later, sand the whole patch with a fine grit sandpaper and feather the edges of the large patch so they will disappear.

6. Wash and finish the area.

When finished sanding, wash the area with water, and when dry, coat with polyurethane. Your job is done and when properly done, will not be visible as a patch except that the area will look new and shiny.

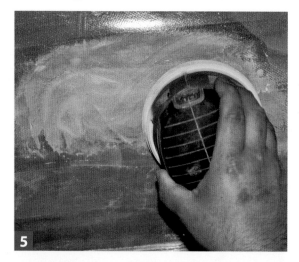

Sand the patch. Once everything is cured, sand the patch, feathering the edge of the large patch so it disappears. When all is smooth, wash the area with clear water and apply a coat of exterior polyurethane.

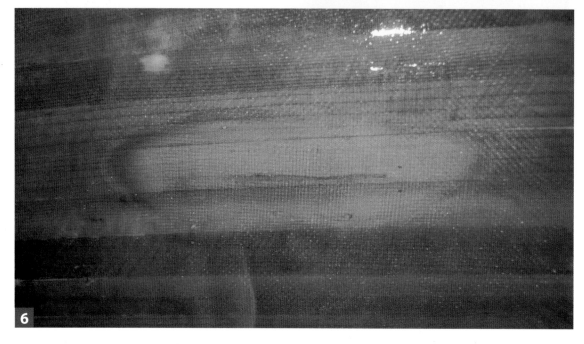

The completed patch. The filled gouge is faintly visible and the wood that was freshly sanded is lighter than the surrounding area, but in time it will darken and the patch will be almost invisible. Right now the bright shiny new coat of varnish does attract the eye.

Repairing an Inside Break

There is another kind of break that can occur when a heavily loaded canoe slides over a smooth rock in the river. The outside of the hull goes undamaged except for perhaps a scratch. However, the offending rock causes the bottom of the canoe to flex upward to the point that the inside fiberglass separates. This is not as serious as an external break, but it does weaken the canoe bottom and causes it to flex more than is desired. Also, in the course of a week-long trip there will probably be water that will get into the break, making it necessary to dry it out before proceeding with the fix.

It isn't necessary to open up the inside break very wide. Just ¼" (6mm) or so to allow the air in will do the trick. When the drying is complete, the area around the break is sanded out to 1½ to 2" (38 to 51mm), same as the outside patch described above. Simply wet out a strip of fiberglass over the break. When cured, feather the edges and coat with polyurethane.

It is only fitting that you make a pair of paddles to match your newly finished canoe.

Chapter 9

Paddles

Ever since I first started building cedar strip canoes in the early 1970s, I wanted to take the next step and build paddles to go along with them. The logical thing was to make them of cedar strips—that being the construction method of the canoe and, besides, there is usually some cedar left over when the canoe is finished.

It wasn't until I discovered and started to use epoxy technology that I was able to make a paddle that would stand up to the rigors of year-in and year-out canoeing on Maine's wilderness rivers. This paddle design has proven itself to be unbelievably tough, lightweight, and durable. My guests and I have given it many years of hard use. I was surprised to discover recently that I was still using one of

the first paddles I ever made using the methods described in this chapter—surprised because most of my guests were new to canoeing. They were likely to use the paddle like a pole to get off a gravel bar or like a pry-bar to extricate themselves when they get stuck on a rock in whitewater. Not to say they are indestructible—we break one now and then. Like most other things, there is wear and tear that has to be repaired occasionally, but I have not found a manufactured paddle to compare to them for strength, lightness, and flexibility. To all this, add the pride of making your own custom paddle, and you have a project that is hard to beat for the serious outdoor person.

Prepare Your Materials

Familiarize yourself with the parts of a paddle (see **Figures 9-1** and **9-2**). Start by making a copy of the full-size patterns (blade, grip, and spine) so you can save the originals for future use. If you will use your patterns more than once, it will be advantageous to make them out of thin plywood, scrap paneling, or whatever. If you know this is a one-time thing, then paper will do. Make the grip area large enough to accommodate whatever grip you wish to make. The grip and shaft is cut to final size when the lamination is complete. The length of the shaft is up to you. Most canoeists agree that a paddle should be long enough to reach somewhere between the standing paddler's chin and nose. I am 6' 1" (1.85m) tall and prefer a paddle 63" (1.6m) long (chin high).

Forms

You will need a piece of plywood—½" (13mm) or thicker—to lay out and tack down your cedar strips. Make an outline of your paddle on this plywood. Cover it with plastic so that the strips will not be glued to it. You will cover the outline with the strips as you glue them up. This is an easy way to ensure the glued-up blade (with the oversize shaft and grip) is large enough to cut out your blade when the glue is dry. Completed blades and the plywood base are shown on page 96.

The jig for gluing up the spines (the core that becomes the handle and the center of the paddle) is shown in **Figure 9-3**. As shown, it will glue up a pair of spines (enough for one paddle) at once. All that is needed besides the jig are the clamps to pull it together. Be sure to use plastic between the spines and between the spines and the jig. The three bolts slide along the slots in the base and keep the

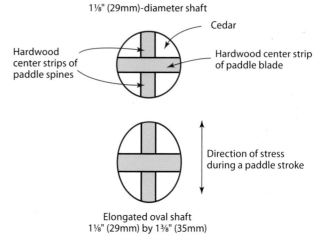

1⅛" (29mm)-diameter shaft

Cedar

Hardwood center strips of paddle spines

Hardwood center strip of paddle blade

Direction of stress during a paddle stroke

Elongated oval shaft
1⅛" (29mm) by 1⅜" (35mm)

Figure 9-2: Shaft cross-section. This drawing represents the cross-section of the shaft of the paddles we are going to build. In order to make the paddle lightweight and strong, a combination of soft wood (cedar) and hardwood are used. The shaded cross represents the hardwood. The X formed by the hardwood provides a strong paddle shaft, yet is much lighter than if solid hardwood were used. If extra strength is desired, the oval (lower) shaft can be used.

slider and the spines from buckling when pressure is applied with the clamps. That's all you will need in the way of forms; the rest of the materials will be part of the paddle itself.

Blade thickness

The paddle blade is to be ¼" (6mm) thick when it is ready to be laminated to the spines. If you have a surface planer available, it is easier to start out with strips that are ⅜" (10mm) thick. Plane the whole thing to ¼" (6mm) after the gluing is done. If your smoothing has to be done by hand or with a sander, then start with strips that are ¼" (6mm), maybe a little more, and then work them down to ¼" (6mm) when dry. The width of the strips is not important. Usually, they are ¾" or ⅞" (19mm or 22mm) because that is the thickness of the boards they are sawn from. Since this is a flat project, wider strips would be perfectly OK.

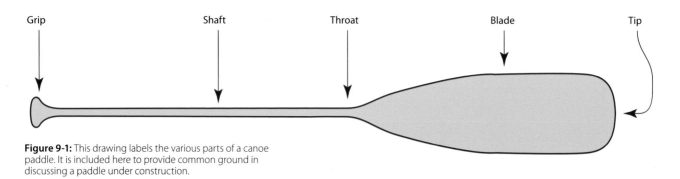

Grip   Shaft   Throat   Blade   Tip

Figure 9-1: This drawing labels the various parts of a canoe paddle. It is included here to provide common ground in discussing a paddle under construction.

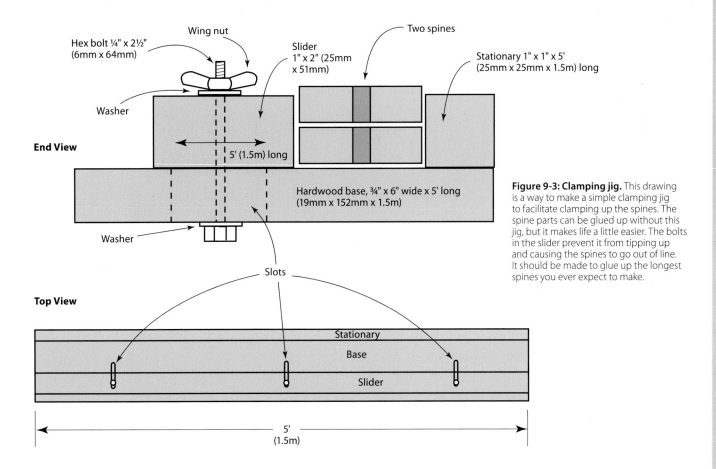

Figure 9-3: Clamping jig. This drawing is a way to make a simple clamping jig to facilitate clamping up the spines. The spine parts can be glued up without this jig, but it makes life a little easier. The bolts in the slider prevent it from tipping up and causing the spines to go out of line. It should be made to glue up the longest spines you ever expect to make.

Spines

The thickness of the spines should be ⅜" or ⁷⁄₁₆" (10mm or 11mm) (your choice) when they are ready to laminate to the blade, so the same thing applies here as to the blade. If you have access to a surface planer, make them ½" or ⁹⁄₁₆" (13mm or 14mm) and plane them to thickness when ready. Otherwise, make them close enough to the finished size that you will not have to remove an excessive amount of wood by hand to prepare them for further lamination. If you think you may need a paddle with a stronger than usual shaft, then you can make the spines a little thicker. You then make the shaft oblong in shape instead of perfectly round (see Figure 9-2). This gives the extra thickness where the pressure is likely to be applied, but adds very little weight.

I should mention here that early on in the development of these paddles we made the spines of solid ash, ⅜" (10mm) thick. This produced a paddle that was strong, somewhat flexible, but a little heavy. If weight is not a factor for you then you can go this route and somewhat simplify the lamination process.

Wood selection

Most of the strips for your paddle will be made from cedar—that makes the paddle light. But there are a few very important strips made of ash, or other strong hardwood—they make your paddle strong. These hardwood strips are arranged to form an *X* in the finished paddle shaft. Look at the cross-section of the paddle shaft in Figure 9-2. The hardwoods I have had good success with are ash, cherry, maple, and birch. The cherry gives a nice contrasting color that fits in well with some paddles. Just keep in mind the goals of lightness, strength, and flexibility.

There is one hardwood strip right in the middle of the paddle blade. Make it the same size as the cedar strips that make up the rest of the blade. The hardwood strip in the spines needs to be the same thickness as the strips, but only ¼" (6mm) wide. This might be a little confusing, because in this reference the thickness is greater than the width. At any rate, you will be using hardwood strips that are ⁹⁄₁₆" (14mm) (or whatever the thickness of your spines are to be) x ¼" (6mm). The ¼" (6mm) hardwood strip for the spines can be seen in Figure 9-2 and in photos 3a and 3b.

Laminating

1. Attach the strips.

The lamination process has to be done in stages. First, you glue up the paddle blade. This is done with ordinary carpenter's glue. These non-waterproof glues can be used here because none of the wood involved will be exposed to water. Lay the ash or other hardwood strip down to establish your paddle centerline and then glue on enough cedar strips to cover your paddle outline. You can staple as you go or place staples only on the outside strips of the blade. It doesn't matter where you staple on the shaft and grip area because these areas are all going to be covered by the spines.

The photo at right shows the stapling being done so as to eliminate staple holes in the finished blade. This is strictly a cosmetic choice and nothing more. The absence of staple holes does make a nice clean surface if you plan any decoration of the blade. Sometimes it is necessary to pull the strips together with a clamp before stapling the outside strip of the paddle blade. The clamp can be left in place until the glue has set up.

2. Complete the drying process.

The glue used for the blade will set up in an hour or so, and at that time it is a good idea to pull it from your form and stand it up to complete the drying process. The reason for doing this is that the glue trapped between the paddle blade and the plastic will not dry very fast. The moisture in the glue will cause the thin strips to warp, causing an extreme cup in the blade. By removing the paddle as soon as possible, and letting the whole thing dry evenly, it will remain flat. Do not pull the staples now, because the glue may not be completely set up.

Attach the strips. Staple the ⅜" (10mm) strips to the mounting board, which has an outline of the paddle with a centerline so you know where to start. The center hardwood strip here is cherry.

Complete the drying process. Avoid leaving the paddles on the board too long. Remove the paddle(s) after about an hour and allow them to finish drying. Here we did a paddle on each side of the mounting board.

3a

Glue up the spines. The spines for one paddle are shown in the clamping jig. Each spine consists of two pieces of cedar ½" (13mm)-thick x ¾" (19mm)-wide and one piece of hardwood ¼" (6mm) x ½" (13mm). To use the clamping jig, it is important that all pieces be uniform in size. There is plastic between the spine and the jig and between the two spines.

3. Apply the spines.

The spines are glued up with epoxy glue made with epoxy resin thickened with cotton fibers. This waterproof glue is needed because the spine will be exposed to the elements. Mix your glue no thicker than necessary to do the job and spread a liberal layer on each strip where they meet. A disposable brush can be used to spread the glue.

Cover both surfaces of the spine parts with epoxy glue before putting them into the clamping jig—this means coating one surface of the cedar strips and both sides of the hardwood center strip. Place the glued-up spine on plastic into the jig and then place another piece of plastic on top of the first spine and repeat the process to make your second spine. When both spines are in place, use several clamps to pull the slider into the spines. Excessive pressure is not necessary and is not recommended. As you tighten the slider, tap the spines with a hammer to ensure they are in alignment. When you do this, simply fold a piece of plastic over the top spine so the glue does not splash or foul up your hammer. Allow the glue of all three components (blade and two spines) to cure overnight or at least 24 hours.

4. Remove the staples and smooth.

Pull the staples from the blade and shaft. Now take all three components and bring them down to the desired thickness with a surface planer, by hand, a sander, or what-have-you. The surfaces need to be as flat as possible to make for good lamination contact as you continue the process.

3b

Clamp the spines. Here is the spine-clamping jig with spines for two paddles.

5

Saw out the blade. Trace the paddle blade by aligning the centerline of the pattern with the center of the hardwood strip. Only cut out the blade at this time. Leave the shaft and grip area as-is for now.

5. Saw out the blade.

Next, trace your blade pattern and saw it out on a band saw, jigsaw, or whatever means you have to do this. Leave the shaft and grip area as-is for now.

Laminating (continued)

6. Shape the ends of the spines.

You are almost ready to laminate the three components together, but first you should work down the pointed ends of the spines so they look like the one in the photo at right. This shaping could be done when the lamination is complete, but it is a lot easier to do beforehand. You will round and thin out only the top side of each spine, leaving the bottom flat for lamination with the blade. A disk sander or belt sander does a quick job of shaping and thinning. You could also use a hand plane or even a rasp.

7. Make the assembly jig.

With the three components of your paddle sized and shaped, you are ready for the final lamination. The simple holding jig shown in the photo below will make it a lot easier to assemble the paddle parts. It can be made of about any scrap wood you might have around the shop.

8. Laminate the paddle.

Before placing the three components into the holding jig, ensure they are all the same width. This usually means cutting down the paddle shaft to match the width of the spines. Also, cut the paddle and the spines to the desired length. The spines should be 12" (305mm) shorter than the paddle. To get the best bond between the spines and the blade/shaft, be sure to coat both components before bringing them together.

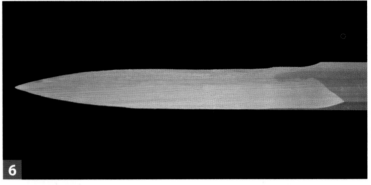

6

Shape the ends of the spines. The end of the spine extends into the paddle blade. Bring the spines to a point, then taper to a knife-edge, leaving one side flat. Since most of the wood to be removed is soft cedar, a variety of tools will do the job. Here we used a belt sander.

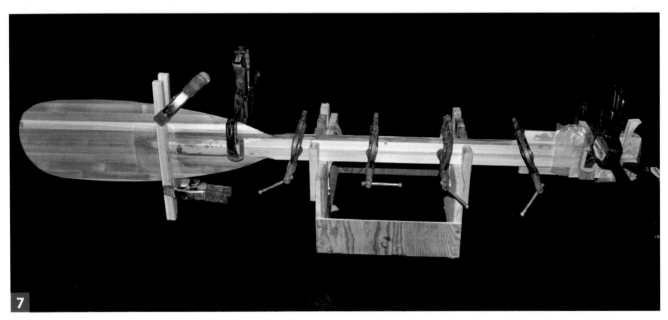

7

Make the assembly jig. Build a holding jig from scrap wood to hold the paddle as it dries. Before the glue-up, saw the shaft of the paddle to the exact same width as the spines. You can see how this would make things easier to line up. It is important that the center of the spines align with the center of the hardwood strip in the paddle. This creates the X shown in Figure 9-2.

9. Clamp the paddle.

After spreading the glue and placing the parts together, you are ready to clamp them. The first couple of clamps are the hardest, as you hold the parts and try to keep them from slipping out of place. Tighten the clamps carefully as you hold them lined up with each other and you will succeed. It is easiest to put a clamp on each end initially, get the alignment correct, and then place the others in between. You have correct alignment at the top when you look down on the top of the grip and see an *X* formed by the hardwood pieces—like that shown in Figure 9-2. The alignment at the blade should have the points of the spines centered on the hardwood strip that runs the length of the paddle blade, shaft, and grip. Do all of your clamping work with the paddle on edge as it is in the holding jig. Finish clamping with enough clamps to bring the parts together without any voids showing anywhere.

The tips (points) of the spines can be clamped firmly against the blade by the clamp system shown in the photo at bottom, right. With this method, you just cover them with plastic or wax paper, put a piece of wood on each side, and then place a clamp on each end of the pieces of wood.

10. Allow the paddle to cure.

When the clamping is finished, allow the paddle to cure right in the holding jig. If you do not leave the paddle to dry on edge, the weight of the clamps will bend the paddle shaft—not the best way to make a bent-shaft paddle. Once the glue has set, the bent shaft will be set as well. If your shaft is not straight in spite of precautions, you can probably correct the situation while the glue is still wet. Simply loosen the clamps slightly, and then give the paddle shaft a little bend to correct the difficulty. You will probably need a helper for this: one person to hold things in place while the other re-tightens the clamps. This correction is seldom necessary.

11. Clean up the glue squeeze-out.

If you plan to shape a grip you will need to glue on the extra wood you will need to shape it out. A scrap piece of cedar is suggested, as it is lightweight and

9a

Clamp the paddle. In the grip area shown here, add pieces to each side of the spines to make the grip wide enough. The dark wood will allow shaping. The other blocks shown beneath the clamps are just to hold pressure and will be removed (they have wax paper between them and the paddle).

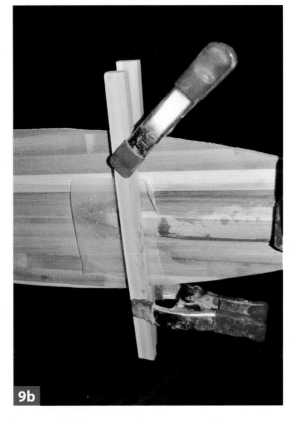

9b

Clamp the spine to the blade. Remove all the glue possible from the surface here so you will not have to sand it off later.

easily shaped. You will also have to add short pieces of wood to each side of the spine in the grip area. Make these the same thickness as the spines. Clean up the squeezed-out glue around the points of the spines where they lay on the paddle blade. It is easier to remove while it is still wet than after it has cured. Leave the paddle to cure for 24 hours or longer.

Shaping the Paddle

1. Sand the paddle.

Remove the clamps, and you now have a very unlikely looking mess that's supposed to become a paddle—but don't worry. Use a sander to clean up the top and bottom so you can mark and cut those areas accurately. Don't worry about the edges where the glue squeezed out; you will cut them away later. Mark the center of the paddle shaft a few inches down from the grip area. This center should be the middle of the ¼" (6mm) hardwood strip. Do the same on the shaft at the throat. Now measure out ½" or ⁹⁄₁₆" (13mm or 14mm) from these marks in both directions so you have 1" or 1⅛" (25mm or 29mm) between the outside marks. Connect these marks with a straightedge on each side of the shaft so you define a 1" or 1⅛" (25mm or 29mm) shaft.

2. Trace in a grip.

With the shaft marked out, select the grip pattern and trace it in the grip area. Adjust the grip pattern so it lines up with the shaft you defined with the straight edge. At the throat, you will need to do a little freehand work on each side to make a smooth, graceful transition from the straight shaft to the rounded blade. When you are satisfied with this and the rest of your marks, go ahead and cut the shaft and grip out with a band saw or whatever means you have to do so.

3. Round over the throat and grip.

Now you have a square paddle shaft that should measure 1" x 1" (25mm x 25mm) or 1⅛" x 1⅛" (29mm x 29mm), and your grip area has its outline shape. At this point, everything from the throat up to and including the grip should be rounded over. If you have a router with a rounding cutter (⅜" [10mm] radius or thereabouts), this will do the job. However, most of the wood you have to remove is cedar, which is soft and almost fun to take off with a rasp.

4. Shape the shaft.

The paddle shaft, of course, should be round or oblong, but you can take artistic license with the grip area or you can copy one of the grips shown in this chapter. In either case this shaping is more artistic than scientific. You can have fun with it by just taking off a little wood and trying it until it feels just right. Once you have the shaft and grip down to the shape you want, you will leave them in the rough and go on to complete the paddle blade. This is done at this point because the resin used in the process of finishing the paddle blade, including the fiberglassing, usually ends up running down the shaft and messing up the finish work you might have done, requiring that the sanding be done all over again to remove it. Better to do all your sanding at once.

2a

Trace in a grip. When the epoxy glue has cured, mark out the width of the shaft. Next, trace out the grip. Where the spine meets the blade, you will need to freehand the line to connect the curve of the blade to the straight line you drew for the shaft. Not difficult!

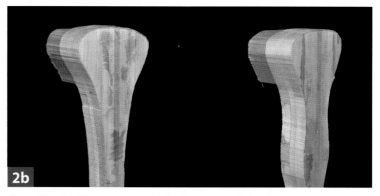

2b

Shape the grip. The grip area is ready for shaping. The shaft will need to be rounded over. You can use a router with a rounding cutter, but lacking that, use an old fashioned wood rasp.

Finishing the Blade

1. Sand the blade.

First sand the paddle blade, removing all glue, pencil marks, machine marks, etc. Initial sanding can be done with 60 grit and then finished up with 80 grit. Finer sanding is unnecessary because the fiberglass covers up any sanding scratches that may be left. At the point where the spine lays on the blade, smooth it out with sandpaper so the junction makes a smooth transition from the flat of the blade to the (previously) rounded shape of the pointed tip of the spine. Even though you carefully removed excess glue from this area when it was still wet, there will be some remaining that has to be taken off. As you do this, be careful not to remove wood that should not be removed. The cedar is soft and can be easily sanded too thin. It is normal to have some glue showing at the junction of the two components when finished, but make sure it feels like a smooth transition as you run your fingers over it.

2. Taper the blade edges.

The tip and edges of your paddle blade are going to be protected by nylon rope. Instructions on how to do this will come a little later. You can use ⅛" or ¼" (3mm or 6mm) braided nylon for the edging. Both are readily available at hardware stores. This blade edging is mentioned here because if you choose to use ⅛" (3mm) braided nylon cord, it is necessary to make the edges of the blade ⅛" (3mm) thick. This is done by tapering the edges from a point about 1½" to 2" (38mm to 51mm) from the edge out to the edge. Take wood off both sides of the blade until the ¼" (6mm) blade tapers gradually down to ⅛" (3mm) at the edges. The taper is quickly done with a power sander and 50-grit sandpaper on the soft cedar. If done smoothly and gradually, this taper will not be apparent to the eye. It is important to have the edge thickness match that of the nylon cord to ensure a good bond between the fiberglass and the nylon cord. Of course, if you use the thicker, ¼" (6mm) nylon, tapering will be unnecessary. I have used both thicknesses with good results. I prefer the ¼" (6mm) braided nylon.

3. Decorate the paddle.

Since prehistoric times, people have been inclined to decorate the tools and other objects that make up their daily lives. In these days of mass production, this practice has diminished except among those who still make their own tools. If you make your own paddle, you are one of those exceptional people. What better way to express yourself, and personalize your paddle, than to do your own design on its broad flat surface? Further, your work will be sealed and protected by the tough and transparent layer of epoxied fiberglass so it will be about as permanent as such things can get. If you wish to do artwork on your paddle, such as woodburning like that shown in the photos on page 108, now is the time to do it. When you finish, proceed with the next step.

4. Prepare to apply the nylon cord.

You will seal the paddle blade and apply the nylon edge in one operation. Find a spot where you can clamp your paddle in an upright position with the grip on the floor (a.k.a., upside down). Cut the nylon rope to length to reach from throat to throat. However, the part of the blade that needs the most protection is the tip, so it is acceptable to cover just that area if you wish. This will require only 12" to 15" (305mm to 381mm) of nylon cord. You will also need two or more straight pins (those used for sewing). You'll see why a little later, but for now leave them sticking up in a piece of scrap wood so they will be easy to pick up with slippery, resin-covered, gloved fingers.

5. Mix some resin.

When everything else is ready to go, put on a pair of protective gloves and mix up a few ounces of resin. Try to estimate enough to cover the blade like varnish and a little extra. The amount needed for these various jobs takes a little practice, but it is always possible to mix up a little more if you run out, so it is OK to be conservative.

Finishing the Blade (continued)

6a

Saturate the cord with resin. A piece of braided nylon rope makes a super protection for the edge of your paddle blade.

6. Saturate the cord.

When the resin and hardener are thoroughly mixed, drop the nylon cord into it and cover it with resin so it will be thoroughly soaked when you are finished with the sealing. The blade is sealed by simply painting on a fairly generous coating of resin (use a throw-away brush). You want it to soak in and seal up the pores of the wood so that the resin used in fiberglassing, later on, will not soak into the wood and leave the fiberglass dry. Apply the sealer to the entire blade up to the throat. This is as far as the fiberglass will go.

Foam Brushes vs Chip Brushes

Foam brushes work fine for two or three minutes to apply resin to a project. After that, the glue holding the brush together starts to break down and the brush falls apart. Throwaway bristle brushes (sold as "chip brushes") are a better choice for longer operations.

6b

Use pins to secure the rope. Using common dressmaker's pins, secure the ends of the rope to the blade near the throat area. Allow it all to cure at least 24 hours, and then remove the pins and taper the ends of the rope so they blend into the throat.

7. Apply the nylon cord to the blade edge.

When the blade is completely covered with resin, including the edges, clamp it in the upright position. Protect the floor beneath the paddle, because it is going to drip. Now take the soaked nylon cord, find the center by holding it up, and carefully place it over the edge of the paddle. You will need to squeeze the nylon a little as you guide it along the edge with your fingers, but do so gently so as not to wring out too much of the resin. Gravity helps you hold the cord in place except where the paddle tapers down to the throat. To take care of this, simply push a straight pin through the nylon into the cedar. If there is extra nylon cord, it is OK to leave a little of the nylon dangling; it has to be trimmed when cured anyway. After a half-hour or so, when the resin gets a little tacky, check the cord to be sure it is still where you want it. Corrections are easily made at this time and the resin is sticky enough so it will not move again.

As mentioned previously, the resin will run down the shaft and will have to be removed, at least most of it, later by sanding. You can minimize this by taping some plastic or wax paper just above the throat to catch this run-off and perhaps save some sanding later on.

8. Fill any voids between the cord and blade.

Because of the difficulty of working around the nylon cord, it is recommended that you allow the sealer and the soaked nylon cord to come to full cure before proceeding. After 24 hours, work can continue on the paddle blade. Remove the pins by twisting and pulling with a pair of pliers. Cut the hardened rope with a tapering cut so it makes a smooth transition to the paddle shaft (throat) or slightly below. If there are voids between the paddle and the nylon cord, they can be filled with an epoxy/silica mix. Make the mixture to a thick paste consistency and fill the voids. The color will match the nylon perfectly. You will have to wait for this mixture to cure before continuing with the sanding.

9. Sand the paddle.

Next you will need to do some sanding to remove bubbles and other irregularities from the surface of the blade, as well as to prepare it for a good mechanical bond with your fiberglass. Don't over-do the sanding; you don't want to remove the sealer coat back into the bare wood.

10. Apply any paper decoration.

If you wish to place some paper with artwork or identification under the fiberglass, now is the time. The photos on pages 107 and 108 show a logo and identification applied in this manner. The logo was made on an ink-jet printer on white paper, but could be made on a photocopier or by hand on any color paper you wish. It is a good idea to experiment with the paper and markers on some scrap before applying it to your paddle. Some are not as compatible with the resin as others. Some papers almost disappear when resin is applied and the result looks like a decal. When your artwork is ready and before you proceed with the fiberglassing, spread a little resin on the spot where the paper will go and put it in place.

11. Drape and trim the fiberglass.

You are ready to start fiberglassing. The cloth will be applied one side at a time; again, gravity will be on your side. Secure the paddle in a horizontal position with the blade not touching anything. Place some plastic under the blade to prevent drips from reaching your floor. The fiberglass cloth can be scraps left over from the canoe building or a lighter weight cloth can be used to shave off a few more ounces. Cut out a piece of 6 ounce, or lighter, fiberglass cloth so that it is about two inches (51mm) larger than the blade. The cloth should reach up to, or almost to, the throat. I have used fiberglass weights from 6 ounces down to 1.5 ounces with good results.

Finishing the Blade (continued)

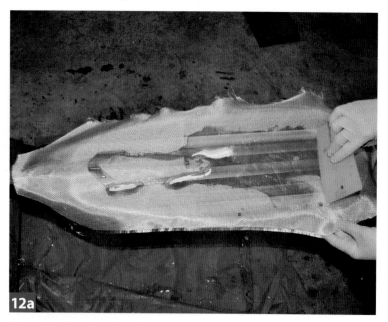

12a

Wet out the fiberglass. Spread the resin with the squeegee and after all is wetted out remove the excess resin. Do only one side of the blade at a time.

12b

Squeegee the spine. Use the edge of the squeegee to ensure there is no bridging of the fiberglass across the valley between the spine and the blade. When this is done, leave it alone to cure. The other side is done the same way.

12. Wet out the fiberglass.

With the cloth in place, pour the remainder of the resin/hardener mix over the cloth. Use a squeegee to spread the resin until the cloth becomes transparent over the entire blade. You may have to be a little careful as you squeegee over the paper not to move it. Pay special attention to the area of the pointed end of the spine. It is easy to leave too much resin in the valley between the blade and the spine, and this allows the cloth to float up. Next, carefully squeegee out excess resin and use it to reinforce the rope edge of the paddle. The best way to do this is to use your squeegee like a snowplow, depositing the excess resin along the edges as you go along. This procedure does two things. First, it will provide resin to fill in any remaining voids or crevices that may exist between the rope and the wood edge of the paddle. Second, it weights down the cloth that extends beyond the paddle edge, ensuring good contact between the cloth and the nylon cord.

Do not try to bring the fiberglass cloth around the edge of the paddle. It will not make that sharp a bend without causing bubbles, and besides, you don't need it. You have that durable nylon rope. All you need is to ensure you have a good bond between the cloth and the rope all the way around.

13. Fill the cloth.

When properly done, the resin wets out the cloth, but does not completely fill it. So, you should be able to see the weave of the cloth and the surface will have a satin (not glossy) look. If you can't see air bubbles anywhere, especially near the edge, the fiberglassing is complete. Leave it for 24 hours, but if you can catch it in the gel stage, this is the best time to put on another thin coat of epoxy to completely fill the cloth and leave a glossy finish. If you cannot do this during the gel stage, then wait and do this fill coat after both sides of the paddle have been fiberglassed.

14. Trim the excess cloth.

The other side of the blade is done exactly like the first. If you did not trim the excess cloth at the gel stage, do so before proceeding. Trim as close as possible to the nylon rope with a sharp knife. Then take a fine wood rasp, and using lengthwise strokes, remove the remainder of the excess cloth back to, but not rasping into, the nylon rope. You will probably find you need to do some fine rasping regardless of when you did the trimming. If you deposited the excess resin near the edge, as mentioned above, there is sufficient resin in this area to achieve a nice rounded edge without rasping into the nylon. Remove any drips that may have accumulated from the previous fiberglassing, then go ahead and fiberglass the remaining side.

15. Feather the edges.

When cured, you will finish up the edge again as instructed in Step 14. At the point where the fiberglass meets wood near the throat, you should feather the fiberglass edge with a fine rasp or sandpaper until the edge cannot be felt when you run your fingers over it. Properly done, feathering makes the edge undetectable when the paddle is complete.

16. Fix any air pockets.

Check the blade, especially the edge where the nylon rope joins wood, for air pockets. If they are tiny they will do no harm, and if you can live with them, will not require further attention. If they are large, take care of them by opening them and filling with thickened resin. The closer to the tip the bubble is, the more potential for trouble, because this is where the paddle receives the most bumping and grinding.

If the filling layer of resin was not applied during the gel stage, don't do it now—the shaft and grip will also receive a coating of waterproofing resin, and you can do it all at once.

Materials and tools needed to make a laminated paddle

Materials:

- 1 piece plywood, ½" (13mm) or more thick, 12" x 72" (.3m x 1.8m)
- 4 pieces ¾" x 2" x 60" (19mm x 51mm x 1.5m) (hardwood preferred)
- Polyethylene plastic (enough to liberally cover the plywood)
- 12 wood screws, #8 x 1¼" (32mm)
- 1 package of ⁹⁄₁₆" (14mm) staples
- 2 or more straight pins (like for sewing)
- 10 (about) cedar strips ⅜" x ¾" (10mm x 19mm), length depends on paddle length. Some will be cut shorter.
- 1 hardwood strip ⅜" x ¾" (10mm x 19mm), same length as cedar strips
- 6 cedar strips ½" x ¾" (13mm x 19mm), length depends on paddle length. Make 12" (305mm) shorter than paddle.
- 2 hardwood strips ¼" x ½" (6mm x 13mm), same length as above.
- Small container of carpenter's glue
- Epoxy and hardener
- Cotton fibers for glue
- Silica
- 6 disposable glue brushes
- Sandpaper, 60, 80 and 120 grits
- 5 feet (1.5m) of ¼" or ⅛" (6mm or 3mm) braided nylon cord
- 3 or 4 throwaway brushes, 2" (51mm)
- 2 pieces 6 ounce (or lighter) fiberglass cloth, approximately 12" x 26" (305mm x 660mm)
- Steel wool, #00
- 1-quart polyurethane varnish with ultra violet filter

Tools:

- Screwdriver
- Surface planer*
- Table saw**
- Stapler (tacker) capable of holding ⁹⁄₁₆" (14mm) staples
- 6 or 8 "C" clamps (more would be better)
- Hammer
- Electric sander*
- Band saw,* jig saw,* or similar method to cut curved lines
- Rasp, 4-in-1
- Hand plane
- Disk sander*
- Carpenter's rule
- Pencil
- Router with ⅜" (10mm) radius rounding bit*
- 1 or 2 plastic squeegees

* Nice to have, but you can get along without these.

** Necessary, but limited use—borrow or beg if you don't have one.

Finishing Up

Apply resin. When you are satisfied with the sanding of the shaft and grip, give the whole paddle a coat of epoxy resin. This will be the fill coat for the fiberglass on the blade and a sealer coat for the shaft and grip.

Apply polyurethane. Thoroughly wash the paddle with clear water, and then give the entire paddle a coat of exterior polyurethane, which has an ultra-violet filter.

1. Sand the shaft and grip.

Now is the time to finish sanding the shaft and grip. Also, give the blade a good sanding to prepare it for the final coat of resin (if it wasn't done during the gel stage). When you are satisfied with the shape, size, and smoothness of the shaft and grip, and you have sanded the blade, you are ready for a layer of resin over the entire paddle, or just the shaft and grip if the blade was previously done.

2. Apply resin.

The resin mixture can be applied with a throwaway brush. Use a generous amount so you end up with a nice glossy surface over the whole paddle—blade, shaft, and grip. You may want to do this process in two steps so you can hang the paddle to cure by a dry part, but I do it all at once. Here's how. In a floor joist overhead, I drove two 3" (76mm) drywall screws so at least two inches (51mm) protrude, and far enough apart so I could hang the wet paddle between them by the grip. There is always a little roughness where the paddle contacts the screws, but that is easily smoothed out. Hang or stand the paddle so that the resin can run off and it will smooth itself out into a nice, glossy, waterproof surface. When the coating reaches the gel state, repeat the coating if needed. Do this as many times as you feel necessary, but one coat is usually sufficient. Remember, the more resin, the heavier the paddle. If you are doing just the shaft and grip at this point, then hang the paddle with the (previously finished) blade end up.

3. Rub down the paddle with steel wool.

When the final coating of resin has cured, you are ready to apply the finishing touch, which is a coating of exterior polyurethane. The epoxy resin has to be protected from the sun's ultra-violet rays, so use an exterior polyurethane varnish with a UV filter. (Most good ones have the UV filter.) Prepare the entire paddle by giving it a good rubdown with steel wool. I use #00 steel wool for this. When finished, the surface should be rather flat or matte looking, but smooth. Now the paddle is ready for the polyurethane.

4. Wash off the paddle with water.

Once the gloss is removed from the entire paddle with steel wool, give the paddle a good washing with plenty of water. For some reason, the epoxy dust causes the polyurethane not to cure properly. So, if you don't want to end up with a sticky mess, do a good job of washing it down. Make sure the paddle is dry before proceeding.

5. Apply polyurethane.

Usually two coats of polyurethane are all that is needed to provide protection and give the paddle an attractive surface. Cosmetic maintenance in the future will require only that you sand a little and apply a little more polyurethane.

That's it; your paddle is finished! I hope you enjoyed building it, and enjoy using it even more. It will provide years of enjoyment and personal satisfaction.

The new paddles are complete. Jason and Kelly Garland show off their new paddles. Now they have to wait for spring to use their new canoe and paddles.

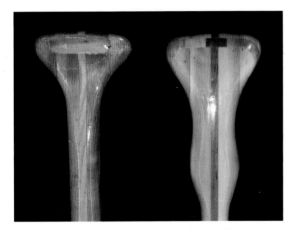

Front grip profiles. Here you can see the front profiles of the paddle grips. Make whichever one seems more comfortable to you.

Paddle identification. Adding a label to the paddle is easily done, and will last for a long time. It will identify the paddle as belonging to you. During my years of guiding, I had several lost paddles returned because I had my name and contact information on them.

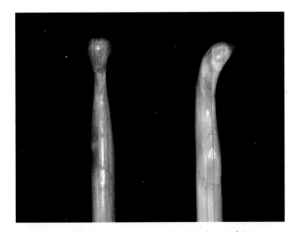

Side grip profiles. Here you can see the side views of the paddle grips.

Finishing Up (continued)

Decorative woodburning. This paddle has a decorative woodburning on it of a scene I liked.

More decorative woodburning. Be creative when adding your decorations—maps, landscape drawings, and more are possible. This paddle features a map of the Allagash Wilderness Waterway.

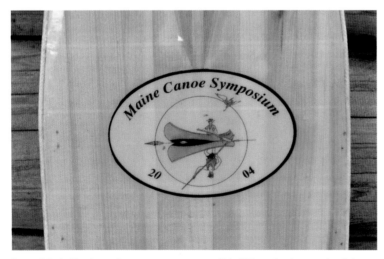

Paper labels. Here's another computer-generated label. The color does tend to fade with time, especially the reds. The canoe in this label was bright red originally.

Appendix: Supply Sources

Please note: There are many more sources of tools and supplies than are listed here. Just make a quick Internet search to find them. I have listed only the sources that I have personally used or have checked out to ensure their reliability and quality.

Fasteners

Jamestown Distributors

17 Peckham Drive
Bristol, RI 02809
800-497-0010
www.jamestowndistributors.com

Brass & bronze fasteners and other boat building supplies

Fiberglassing supplies

Raka, Inc.

3490 Oleander Ave.
Ft. Pierce, Florida 34982
772-489-4070
www.raka.com

Epoxy and a complete line of fiberglassing tools & supplies

WEST System

Gougeon Brothers, Inc
102 Patterson Ave.
P.O. Box 665
Bay City, MI 48707
866-937-8797
www.westsystem.com

Epoxy and a complete line of fiberglassing tools & supplies

Lumber

Tweedie Lumber, Inc.

188 Brooks Rd.
Thorndike, Maine 04986
207-568-3632
bruce@tweedielumber.com

Quality eastern white cedar, will ship

Newfound Woodworks, Inc.

67 Danforth Brook Road
Bristol, NH 03222
603-744-6872
www.newfound.com

A good source of finished wood strips if you don't want to make your own.

Cane for Seats

Connecticut Cane and Reed Company

P.O. Box 762
Manchester, CT 06045
860-646-6586
www.caneandreed.com

Plastic cane and seat making supplies

H.H. Perkins Co.

222 Universal Drive South
North Haven, CT 06473
800-462-6660
www.hhperkins.com

Plastic cane and seat making supplies

Special Tools

MLCS

P.O. Box 165
Huntingdon Valley, PA 19006
800-533-9298
www.mlcswoodworking.com

Router bits for cutting beads and flutes in canoe strips

Index

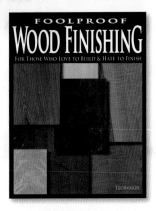

COPYEDITOR: Lynda Jo Runkle
COVER DESIGNER: Troy Thorne
DESIGNER: Lindsay Hess
EDITOR: Kerri Landis
PROOFREADER: Paul Hambke
INDEXER: Jay Kreider